HEROES

∽IN∽

BLACK
HISTORY

DAVE + NETA JACKSON

HEROES  IN BLACK HISTORY

True Stories from the Lives of Christian Heroes

BETHANY HOUSE PUBLISHERS

Published by Bethany House Publishers
11400 Hampshire Avenue South
Bloomington, MN 55438

Bethany House Publishers is a division of
Baker Publishing Group, Grand Rapids, Michigan.

Printed in the United States of America by Bethany Press International, Bloomington, MN. November 2009, 2nd printing

Library of Congress Cataloging-in-Publication Data

Jackson, Dave.
    Heroes in Black History : true stories from the lives of Christian heroes / Dave and Neta Jackson.
        p.   cm.
    "Heroes in Black History is a special-edition compilation of brand-new material as well as existing material pulled from Dave and Neta Jackson's Hero Tales, Vols I–IV"—T.p. verso
    Summary: "Presents biographies of influential Christians from black history who worked courageously to spread the Gospel and effect social change"—Provided by publisher.

    ISBN 978-0-7642-0556-9 (pbk. : alk. paper)   1. Christians, Black—Biography—Juvenile literature.   I. Jackson, Neta. II. Title.
    BR1702.J33   2008
    270.092'396—dc22
[B]
                                                                                                    2007045868

To our friends and prayer partners,

Carlton and Karen Evans

Contents

Harriet Tubman: **Conductor on the Underground Railroad**   9
Blow to the Forehead—Compassion   *11*
Liberty . . . or Death—Joy   *14*
"Wanted: Dead or Alive!"—Perseverance   *17*

Samuel Morris: **Evangelist From Africa**   *21*
The "Sheriff" of the Three-Masted Ship—Peacemaker   *23*
Taking New York—Boldness   *26*
Take Heart!—Encouragement   *29*

Amanda Smith: **American Evangelist to the World**   *33*
Going to the Fair—Obedience   *35*
Two Dollars for India—Trust   *38*
The Best Way to Fight—Forgiveness   *44*

Charles Albert Tindley: **Prince of Preachers**   *45*
Heaven's Christmas Tree—Hope   *47*
"No Charge"—Compassion   *51*
The Singing Preacher—Praise   *54*

George Washington Carver: **The Man Who Saved the South From Poverty**   *59*
"Be Like Libby"—Perseverance   *61*
Most Weeds Have a Purpose—Resourcefulness   *64*
The School on Wheels—Service   *67*

William Seymour: **"Father" of Modern Pentecostals**   *71*
The Headless Phantom—Discernment   *73*
Washing Away the Color Line—Reconciliation   *76*
Many Languages, Many Gifts, One Gospel—Faithfulness   *79*

Mary McLeod Bethune: **Teacher of Head, Hands, and Heart**   *83*
"But . . . Where's the School?"—Faith   *85*
No Such Thing as a Menial Task—Diligence   *89*
" 'Whosoever' Means You!"—Dignity   *92*

Thomas A. Dorsey: **The Father of Gospel Music** **97**
Taming a Wildcat—Surrender *100*
"Take My Hand, Precious Lord"—Submission *103*
"When I've Done My Best"—Excellence *106*

Eliza Davis George: **Liberia's American "Mother"** **111**
Two Hundred Miles by Ankle-Express—Perseverance *113*
Snip and Stitch—Encouragement *116*
"Son, Take It"—Sacrifice *119*

Dr. Martin Luther King Jr.: **Civil Rights Leader** **123**
The Birth of a Dream—Dignity *126*
The Power of Turning the Other Cheek—Nonviolence *129*
"I'm So Happy That You Didn't Sneeze!"—Self-Sacrifice *133*

John Perkins: **A Man Hate Couldn't Stop** **137**
One Small Push for Justice—Wisdom *139*
Beaten in the Brandon Jail—Forgiveness *142*
Black and White Together—Reconciliation *145*

Festo Kivengere: **Africa's Apostle of Love** **149**
No Place to Hide—Surrender *151*
A Language Anyone Can Understand—Repentance *154*
"I Love Idi Amin"—Love *157*

Ricky and Sherialyn Byrdsong: **Coaching Kids in the Game of Life** **161**
Windy-City Panhandler—Advocate *163*
From Tragedy to Triumph—Victory *166*
The Missing Shoes—Generosity *169*

Ben Carson: **The Brain Surgeon They Called "Dummy"** **173**
One Shiny Rock—Vision *175*
Crabs in a Bucket—Wisdom *178*
It's No Accident—Victory *181*

List of Character Qualities **185**

HARRIET TUBMAN

Conductor on the Underground Railroad

Araminta Ross was born a slave around 1820 on a Maryland plantation owned by Edward Brodas. "Minty," as she was called, was taught Bible stories, gospel songs, and spirituals by her deeply religious parents. But in the tense years just before the Civil War, slaves were not allowed to gather in groups, not even for church.

The Brodas plantation was falling on hard times. Sometimes Edward Brodas "hired out" his slaves to make ends meet—including little Minty. But she got sent back home each time because people thought she was "stubborn" or "stupid." Deciding that Minty was hopeless at housework, Brodas put her to work in the fields, which was much harder—but also much more to her liking. By age eleven, she had shed the nickname Minty. Folks now called her Harriet, after her mother.

In 1844, at the age of twenty-four, Harriet married a free Negro named John Tubman. When she talked to her husband about running away, he said he would tell her master if she tried it! But Harriet couldn't give up the hope of freedom. She had heard about an "underground railroad" that took slaves to freedom in the northern states.

In 1849, she knew the time had come. She traveled only at night, using all her knowledge of the woods to make her way north. At each friendly "station" or stop on the way, she was told where to go next.

When she arrived in Pennsylvania, she was excited by her new freedom. But instead of sitting back and enjoying freedom for herself, Harriet went back to lead other slaves to freedom—over three hundred during her lifetime.

During the Civil War, she was recruited as a "nurse" and a spy for the Union Army. But even though she was greatly respected, she never received any of the army pay owed her.

After the war, when slavery finally ended, Harriet began a home for the sick, poor, and homeless in Auburn, New York. She died there in 1913 at the age of ninety-three.

Compassion

BLOW TO
THE FOREHEAD

Thirteen-year-old Harriet saw the silent, moody slave slip away from the cornhusking bee on the Brodas plantation even before the overseer did. But within minutes, she heard the overseer shout, "Hey! You, there—stop!"

But the slave didn't stop. He started to run, with the overseer fast on his heels. Not quite understanding why she did so, Harriet dropped the corn she was husking and followed. Something bad was going to happen. She had to do something. A slave who tried to run away and was caught was beaten severely—and then sold down South to a chain gang.

The runaway tried to hide in a little country store at the crossroads, but the overseer went in after him. The slave was cornered, breathing heavily, and the overseer threatened to whip him then and there.

"You, girl!" the angry overseer shouted at Harriet when she appeared in the doorway. "Help me tie this man up."

Harriet didn't move. Realizing she was giving him a chance, the slave darted past Harriet and started to run. In an effort to stop him, the overseer grabbed a two-pound weight and threw it at the runaway. But in that same moment, Harriet stepped in the way.

The weight struck her full in the forehead, knocking her backward. She was unconscious for days; then she slipped in and out of a stupor for months. But as Harriet slowly recovered, a constant prayer was on her lips—for her master: "Change his heart, Lord."

The wound finally healed, but for the rest of her life, Harriet suffered terrible headaches and a strange "sleeping sickness" that made her suddenly black out for a few minutes or even a few hours.

As winter turned to spring, a rumor went around the slave quarters: The master was going to sell Harriet to the next slave trader who came along for her part in letting the slave escape. Angry, her prayer changed. "Lord, if you're never going to change Massa Brodas' heart, then kill him, Lord! Take him out of the way."

Within weeks, Edward Brodas became ill. He died even before the new tobacco crop had been planted. Horrified, Harriet thought she had killed him!

Edward Brodas had promised Harriet's parents that they would have their freedom when he died. But when his will was read, it said only that none of his slaves could be sold outside the state of Maryland.

Even when she heard this terrible news, Harriet felt sorry that her master had died without changing his heart. She often said, "I would give the world full of silver and gold to bring that poor soul back. . . . I would give myself. I would give everything!"

Compassion is bearing someone else's burden as if it were your own.

FROM GOD'S WORD:

By helping each other with your troubles, you truly obey the law of Christ (Galatians 6:2).

LET'S TALK ABOUT IT:

1. In what way did Harriet have compassion for the runaway slave? In what way did she have compassion for her master?
2. How is it possible to have compassion both for people who suffer and for people who cause the suffering?
3. What is the "law of Christ" that we fulfill when we help each other with troubles? (See Galatians 5:14.)

Joy

LIBERTY . . . OR DEATH

John," whispered Harriet to her new husband, "you already have your freedom, but I want to be free, too. Why don't we run away up north to one of the free states where—"

"That's foolishness!" interrupted John Tubman, a free black man who had asked her owner for permission to marry the twenty-four-year-old Harriet. He didn't want any trouble. "If I hear you talking that way again, I'll tell your master!"

Harriet was hurt. If John loved her, wouldn't he want her to be free, too? She never brought up the subject again, but she thought about it all the time.

She had heard about the Underground Railroad that took slaves to freedom in the northern states. "There is one of two things I have a right to," she told herself. "Liberty or death. If I cannot have one, I will have the other, for no man will take me alive. I will fight for my liberty as long as my strength lasts, and when the time comes for me to go, the Lord will let them take me."

One night, she silently made her way through the woods to the home of a white Quaker woman who had once told her, "If you ever need help, come to me." There she learned that the Underground Railroad was not a railroad at all, but a network of "stations"—farmers and townspeople who were willing to hide slaves and help them reach freedom.

Harriet traveled only at night. At each friendly station, she was told where to go next. Along the way, she traveled in a wagon under a load of vegetables, was rowed up the Choptank River by a man she had never seen before, was hidden in a haystack, spent a week in a potato hole in a cabin that belonged to a family of free blacks, was hidden in the attic of a Quaker family, and was befriended by German farmers.

Harriet's daily prayer became, "Lord, I'm going to hold steady on to you, and you've got to see me through." Still suffering from her head injury, she sometimes fell asleep right on the road, but somehow she managed to escape being discovered.

Near Wilmington, Delaware, Harriet had been told to hide in a grave-yard. A man came wandering through muttering, "I have a ticket for the railroad." This man disguised Harriet in workman's clothes and took her to the house of Thomas Garrett, a famous Quaker who worked hard to end slavery. Garrett, who had a shoe shop, gave her new shoes and fancy women's clothes and drove her in his buggy north of Wilmington. Then he gave Harriet, who couldn't read or write, a paper with the word *PENNSYLVANIA* written on it so she could recognize the sign when she crossed the state line.

Harriet finally crossed into Pennsylvania—a free state. She had trav-eled a total of ninety miles. In spite of her tiredness, joy flooded her from head to toe. She was free! The feeling was like nothing she'd ever felt before.

Harriet looked wonderingly at her hands to see if she was the same person. "There was such a glory over everything," she said later. "The sun came like gold through the trees and over the fields, and I felt like I was in heaven."

Joy is a gift from God, a taste of what it will be like in heaven.

FROM GOD'S WORD:

Crying may last for a night, but joy comes in the morning (Psalm 30:5b).

LET'S TALK ABOUT IT:

1. Why do you think John Tubman didn't want to help his wife run away to freedom?
2. Try to imagine what Harriet felt like when she reached freedom. How would you describe it?
3. What kinds of experiences here on earth give us a taste of the joy waiting for us in heaven?

Perseverance

"WANTED: DEAD OR ALIVE!"

Shhh," Harriet Tubman hissed. The farmhouse in the clearing was dark. Where was the signal light that was supposed to welcome them?

Harriet had lost track of how many trips she'd made back to Maryland to rescue slaves. She had gone back the first few times to lead members of her own family to freedom. Then she kept going back—taking any slave willing to risk the hard road to freedom. But it was dangerous. Posters with Harriet's name and picture were posted all over Maryland: "Wanted: Harriet Tubman—dead or alive! Reward $40,000." The runaways had to sleep in the woods during the day and travel only at night.

Tonight the runaway slaves (Harriet called them her passengers) were exhausted and hungry. Their feet dragged slower and slower. Now they had reached the next station on the Underground Railroad. Creeping closer, Harriet knocked at the farmhouse door.

The door opened a crack. "Who is it?" whispered a frightened voice.

Harriet gave the password: "A friend with friends."

"The slave-catchers searched my house yesterday," said the frightened voice. "Go away! Quickly!" And the door slammed shut.

The runaway slaves were dismayed. They were so tired, so hungry . . . how could they keep going?

But they had to keep going. They stumbled back into the woods. Hunger gnawed at their bellies. Their feet were bruised. When the sun started to come up, they crawled under the bushes and leaves and fell into an uneasy sleep.

But Harriet couldn't sleep. She knew the runaways were too tired to go much farther. They needed a friend, someone to help them. Over and over she prayed to her heavenly Friend: "Lord, I'm going to hold steady on to you, and you've got to see us through."

As night fell once more, she heard a voice. Someone was coming! The others shrank back under the bushes, fear in their eyes. Then they heard a man's voice mumbling to himself, "My wagon stands in the barnyard across the way. The horse is in the stable. The harness hangs on a nail." Still mumbling, the man kept walking and was soon gone.

Harriet closed her eyes in relief. God *had* sent a friend to help them!

When it was dark, Harriet crept by herself to the edge of the woods. Sure enough, there was a wagon standing in a barnyard. In the barn was a sturdy horse. And in the wagon were a stack of blankets and baskets of food.

Quickly harnessing the horse, Harriet drove the wagon back to get her passengers.

"Praise God! Thank you, Jesus!" they cried as they crawled into the wagon. Harriet slapped the reins on the horse's rump. They were back on the road to freedom!

Harriet kept going South, leading more than three hundred slaves to freedom. At the end of her life, she said, "On my Underground Railroad, I never ran my train off the track, and I never lost a passenger."

Perseverance is continuing to do what is right,
even when you get tired or run into problems.

FROM GOD'S WORD:

We must not become tired of doing good. We will receive our harvest of eternal life at the right time if we do not give up (Galatians 6:9).

LET'S TALK ABOUT IT:

1. Why do you think Harriet risked going back to help others once she had reached freedom?
2. What did Harriet do when she felt too tired to go on?
3. Do you sometimes get tired of doing good? (Talk about it.) What can you do to "persevere"?

SAMUEL MORRIS

Evangelist From Africa

Prince Kaboo was born in 1872 in Liberia (western Africa). His father was king of the Kru tribe during a war with the neighboring Grebos. The Grebos won.

Because the king could not pay his war taxes, he had to surrender Kaboo as a "pawn" until the debt was paid. This happened once when Kaboo was a small child, but his father was able to free him quickly. However, when Kaboo was a young teenager, new fighting broke out. His people were defeated, and he was again taken as a pawn.

When Kaboo's father was unable to pay his ransom, the Grebos began torturing Kaboo to force his father to pay.

Once when Kaboo was being whipped, a blinding light flashed, and a voice from heaven said, "Rise up and run."

Strength returned to Kaboo's wounded body, and he ran into the jungle. Grebo warriors followed him until dark.

But nighttime did not stop Kaboo. God provided a miraculous light to guide him. During the day, he slept in hollow logs. Finally, he arrived at the town of Monrovia, where missionaries told him about Jesus.

When Kaboo heard the story of Saul's conversion on the road to Damascus, he exclaimed, "That happened to me, too. A light flashed, and God spoke from heaven."

Kaboo (called Samuel Morris by then) went to the United States to study God's Word at Taylor University in Fort Wayne, Indiana. Whenever he spoke at the university or while traveling, powerful revivals broke out. Many people gave their hearts to Jesus.

However, weeks of being tortured had weakened Samuel's body. During the harsh winter of 1892-93 he became ill. He died that spring.

Though Samuel's death at the age of twenty seemed tragic, God used it to inspire many students to be missionaries in Samuel's place. A Taylor University Bible School was even started in Africa.

Peacemaker

THE "SHERIFF" OF
THE THREE-MASTED SHIP

The tough sea captain didn't want this young African boy on board his ship.

"But my Father told me you would take me to New York," said Samuel Morris. "I'm going there to learn about the Holy Spirit."

"Get away from here," the captain growled. He kicked Samuel.

But the next day, the boy was back, declaring confidently that he was going on the ship. Samuel wouldn't give up, so finally the captain gave in.

Samuel had no skills as a sailor, and because of his black skin, he was hated by the crew. But one crew member accepted him. The captain's cabin boy had just been seriously hurt and could not get up. Samuel knelt down and prayed for him. Immediately, the young man rose to his feet, completely healed.

One day when most of the crew was drunk, a fight broke out. A large Malay man thought someone had insulted him; he charged at his shipmates, swinging a cutlass.

Samuel stepped in his way and said, "Don't kill! Don't kill!"

The Malay man hated blacks and had killed others in the past. He'd sworn to kill Samuel, too. But for some reason, he slowly lowered his weapon and went below deck. Every man on deck was shocked. They knew how violent the man was. Samuel had a power stronger than the meanest sailor!

Unlike the sheriffs of the American "Old West," Samuel didn't threaten anyone in order to restore peace. Instead, he immediately began praying for all the men who were fighting. Before the captain knew what he was doing, he was praying, too, and confessing his own sins. That same day, he asked Jesus to be his Savior.

By the next morning, the murderous Malay was so sick that no one expected him to live. But Samuel was not discouraged. He went to visit the man and prayed for him, even though this was the man who had said he would kill him. God answered Samuel's prayer. The Malay man recovered immediately. From that time on, he treated Samuel like a brother.

Samuel started holding church services on deck, and every man happily took part. Samuel's faith had changed the whole spirit of the ship.

Years later, when the captain of this ship learned that Samuel Morris had died, he was so sad that he could not speak for some time. Then he said that most of the old crew were still on board and excited to find out about their beloved hero and minister. After all, he had changed life on that ship. Before he came aboard, no one had ever prayed out loud, but after Samuel shared the Gospel with them, they became like one family—a family that could talk to their Father.

Peacemaking sometimes means being willing to risk your safety in order to prevent harm to others.

FROM GOD'S WORD:

People who work for peace in a peaceful way plant a good crop of right-living (James 3:18).

LET'S TALK ABOUT IT:

1. At first, why didn't the sailors welcome Samuel Morris as part of the crew? What changed their minds?
2. Why did Samuel risk his own safety to stop the man with the cutlass?
3. Tell about a time when you tried to break up a fight or settle an argument between two people.

Boldness

TAKING NEW YORK

The tired missionary had been talking to Samuel Morris at the mission in Monrovia for hours. "If you want to learn any more about the Holy Spirit," she finally said, "then you'll have to go see Stephen Merritt in New York."

So, at about the age of nineteen, Samuel left his home in Liberia and talked his way on board a ship bound for New York.

Besides being a Bible teacher and well-known preacher, Merritt ran a mission for homeless people. When Samuel stepped off the ship and onto the dock in New York, he boldly said to the first person he met, "Please take me to Stephen Merritt." He had no idea how big New York City was!

But even though the mission was on the other side of town, this man had stayed there often and agreed to show Samuel the way.

When Samuel met Stephen Merritt, he explained, "I have come from Africa to talk with you about the Holy Spirit."

"I'm sorry, son," said Merritt, "but right now I'm going out the door to a prayer meeting. Wait in the mission. When I get back, I'll see about a place for you to sleep."

Stephen Merritt forgot about his new guest until he returned late that night. In the mission, he found Samuel with seventeen men around him. They were some of the toughest street men Merritt had ever housed, but Samuel had them on their knees praying and asking for God's forgiveness.

That Friday evening was just the beginning.

On Saturday, Merritt was scheduled to speak at a funeral. He invited Samuel to go along with him, thinking he would show this bright young African around the city and introduce him to some important people.

After seeing the opera house, Central Park, and several other sights, Samuel said, "Stephen Merritt, do you ever pray in this coach?"

"Oh yes," said Merritt, "I often find it a fine place to pray as I drive about."

"Good," said Samuel, and he *knelt* down and began to pray. "Dear Father, I have come all the way from Africa to talk to Mr. Merritt about your Holy Spirit, but all he wants to do is show me other things. Please take these *things* out of his heart so he cannot talk of anything except your Holy Spirit."

Merritt was shocked, but their conversation changed. As they talked, the power of the Holy Spirit seemed to fill the coach. At the funeral, the message Merritt had prepared left his mind, and instead he preached what the Holy Spirit gave him to say. When it was over, many people gave their lives to Jesus.

Later, Merritt said that even though important church leaders had prayed over him, he had never felt the power of the Holy Spirit so strongly as he had in that coach with Samuel.

On Sunday, Merritt invited Samuel to speak to a Sunday school class of young people. At first they laughed. But when Merritt returned to the room after a short time away, he found the young people crying over their past sins and praying to God for forgiveness.

Those young people organized the Samuel Morris Missionary Society, which helped support Samuel when he left New York to study at Taylor University.

Boldness requires going after a goal single-mindedly.

FROM GOD'S WORD:

Ask, and God will give to you. Search, and you will find. Knock, and the door will open for you (Matthew 7:7).

LET'S TALK ABOUT IT:

1. How did God answer Samuel Morris's search to know more about the Holy Spirit?
2. Who benefitted from Samuel's boldness?
3. What is a goal in your life that you think God would bless if you went after it boldly?

Encouragement

TAKE HEART!

I am Samuel Morris. I have just come from Africa with a message for your people," the young student said as he stepped onto the church platform.

The surprised minister didn't know what to do. He would not usually let a stranger take over his service. But something about the young African caused him to agree.

It was Samuel's first Sunday in Fort Wayne, Indiana, where he had come to attend Taylor University. He did not have a prepared sermon. He simply started praying and encouraged the people to do the same. Soon the whole congregation was on their knees praying and worshiping God. "It was the most joyful service we ever had," said the grateful minister later.

After that, Samuel spoke in other churches—even in a roller-skating rink. People came from all over to hear him talk about God.

Though he was just learning to read, those who heard him speak were surprised at the freshness and strength of his messages. One said, "He spoke for forty minutes in a quiet yet earnest style, simple and natural as a child. Everyone was interested."

At school, Samuel did not eat any food or drink any water from Thursday night until Saturday morning. He had figured out that God had miraculously rescued him from his Grebo captors on a Friday. So he saved that day for praying—"talking to my Father," as he called it.

As other people heard about this young African at the school, they gave money to a "faith fund" for his costs. (Even after Samuel's death, that fund continued to grow, helping one hundred needy students who were preparing for mission work.)

During Samuel's time at Taylor University, the people in charge of the school almost closed it because there was not enough money to pay the bills.

"Take heart," said Samuel, "and pray." Inspired by his faith, the board members turned to God for help.

At their next meeting, one board member suggested that if the school couldn't afford to remain in Fort Wayne, it should move to Upland. Move the whole school? That seemed impossible! But with Samuel's encouragement, the board member raised enough money *within one day* to purchase new land and move the school.

Samuel's inspiration meant new life for the school. But at age twenty, Samuel became ill because of the injuries he had received as a boy in Africa. After his death, hundreds attended his funeral, packing the church and spilling out into the street. In Samuel, many of them had seen and learned more about faith and the power of God to save people than they had ever known before.

Encouraged by Samuel's example, many students volunteered as missionaries in his place. And for years to come, missions was an important focus of the school—until hundreds had gone overseas to be missionaries.

Of Samuel Morris, the president of the university said, "He thought he was coming over here to prepare himself for his mission to his people, but his coming was to prepare Taylor University for her mission to the whole world."

Encouragement helps others do more than they think they can do.

FROM GOD'S WORD:

You should meet together and encourage each other. Do this even more as you see the day coming (Hebrews 10:25).

LET'S TALK ABOUT IT:

1. How did Samuel Morris encourage the first church he went to in Fort Wayne?
2. How did his encouragement save the university?
3. Tell about a time when someone encouraged you to do more than you thought you could do.

AMANDA SMITH

American Evangelist to the World

Amanda Berry was born into slavery in Maryland in 1837. Her father, Samuel Berry, managed to buy his freedom, as well as that of his wife and children. Praising God for deliverance, the family moved to Pennsylvania, a free state, where their home became a station on the Underground Railroad for runaway slaves.

Though raised by strong Christian parents, Amanda had not yet decided to follow Jesus when she married at seventeen. Her husband was a heavy drinker, but the difficult marriage ended when he was killed during the Civil War. Amanda, meanwhile, experienced the "saving grace of Jesus" during a Baptist revival. Now her deepest desire was to share God's good news of salvation.

Amanda then married James Smith, an aspiring preacher, but her hopes for a Christian home were disappointed. James grew less interested in spiritual things and was often away from home. She gave birth to five children during her two marriages, but only one daughter, Maizie, lived past infancy. When James died in 1869, Amanda, only thirty-two, never married again, even though it meant supporting herself and her child by taking in washing and ironing.

Amanda had a beautiful voice and often sang and spoke her message of salvation and "sanctification," or holiness, in both black and white churches and at camp meetings. She faced many barriers because she was not only a "woman preacher," but a "colored" woman preacher. But her spirit was always gracious, not pushing in where she was not wanted. In everything, she tried to be obedient to the leading of the Holy Spirit.

In time, her evangelistic work took her to England, India, Africa, and back to the United States, where she founded the Amanda Smith Orphans Home near Chicago, Illinois. A humble woman of great faith and prayer, Amanda Berry Smith went to be with her Lord in 1915 at the age of seventy-eight.

Obedience

GOING TO THE FAIR

Amanda Smith walked wearily toward her home at 135 Amity Street in New York. Her back ached from bending over the washtub all day. She would make herself a small supper, spend some quiet time in prayer, and go to bed.

"Oh, Sister Smith! Wait one moment!" Sister Johns, a friend from church, was waving at her. "Are you going to the fair tonight?"

Amanda had forgotten about the fair. Several churches were putting on a fund-raising event. Everyone seemed to enjoy the merry crowds, especially the young people. But Amanda shook her head. "No. I'm very tired tonight."

"Oh." Sister Johns' face fell. "I have two tickets to give away. I was hoping you could use them."

Oh, Lord, Amanda thought. *Are you trying to tell me something?* Amanda never made a decision without asking God what He wanted her to do. "Well," she said reluctantly, "give me the tickets. If God wants me to go to the fair, I'll use them."

As Amanda made her tea and supper, she prayed about the tickets. In her heart, God was making it clear that He wanted her to go. But why? She didn't know, but if God wanted her to do a thing, it was always for some purpose.

She tucked some tracts about salvation and holiness in her coat pocket and walked back out into the November night. The hall where the fair was being held was brightly lit. The crowds buzzed around Amanda, but she felt alone and useless.

"Lord, help me," she prayed. "Show me what you want me to do."

Standing at the top of the stairs where people were coming into the fair, she saw two young men taking the steps two at a time, laughing and shoving as boys do. One of the boys rarely came to church and made no claim to having faith. "Speak to that young man," the Holy Spirit seemed to say.

"Charlie!" Amanda said as he was about to pass by. "I have a tract I'd like you to read."

The boy stopped. "How do, Mrs. Smith?" he asked politely. He took the tract and shrugged. "I grew up with this stuff all my life, you know. Guess I have time to have a bit of fun before I become a sober-faced deacon." His friend snickered.

Amanda patted him on the arm. "It's not about becoming a deacon, Charlie. It's about your soul's salvation. Read it, son, read it."

"All right, Mrs. Smith, whatever you say!" Charlie laughed and ran off with his friend.

Suddenly, Amanda realized she could go home. That was it. That was why God wanted her to come to the fair. To give a tract to Charlie.

Several days later, Amanda was once again heading home carrying a load of wash to do that night. "Sister Smith! Did you hear?" a voice called. It was Sister Johns, hurrying to speak to her. "Young Charlie was found dead in his bed this morning. Can you imagine? Why, I saw him at the fair not three days ago, healthy as a colt!"

As Sister Johns chattered on, Amanda's heart was both sad and glad. *Oh, Lord,* she prayed, *thank you for giving me the strength to obey you the other night and go to the fair. I don't know whether Charlie responded to the message in the tract or not. I leave that in your hands. My job was to obey.*

*Obedience is the willingness to respond to God's still, small voice,
even when it goes against our own plans.*

FROM GOD'S WORD:

[Jesus] replied, "Blessed rather are those who hear the word of God
and obey it" (Luke 11:28 NIV).

LET'S TALK ABOUT IT:

1. Why did Amanda Smith pray about whether to go to the fair, even though her back hurt and her feet were tired?
2. Concerning Charlie, what part was Amanda's job? What part was God's job?
3. Can you think of a time you felt God was asking you to do something, but you didn't feel like doing it? What did you do? What happened?

Trust

TWO DOLLARS FOR INDIA

Amanda Smith scooted over on the bench under the big tent to make room for two white ladies dressed in elegant hats and black lace shawls. *What a blessing,* Amanda thought, *that rich and poor, black and white, can come together at camp meeting time to hear such fine preaching for a whole week.* This morning her daughter, Maizie, was at the young people's meeting, but Amanda was eager to hear the missionary woman from India speak.

Amanda's heart ached as the missionary showed the small wooden idols that many people worshiped in India. *How I wish I could tell them the Good News about Jesus!* she thought.

At the end of the meeting, the missionary asked people to give money to help support Bible teachers in India. *I'd give twenty dollars if I could!* thought Amanda. But all she had was two dollars—and that was to buy a new pair of shoes for Maizie.

"Give the two dollars," the Holy Spirit nudged.

"Ho, ho!" the devil seemed to whisper in her other ear. "Won't you look like a fool in front of these rich ladies giving just two dollars."

Just then the elegant ladies beside Amanda stood up. *Oh, good,* she thought. *They'll be able to give a lot of money, and the missionary won't need my two dollars.* But to her dismay, the women walked out of the tent without giving anything. Several more women got up and left.

"Give the two dollars," the Spirit said again.

"Your child needs shoes," the devil reminded her. "Your first duty is to your child."

Amanda stood up. Maybe she, too, should just leave like the other women. Instead, she found herself moving toward the missionary speaker. "Will two dollars help bring the Gospel to the people in India?" she asked.

"Of course! God bless you," said the missionary warmly.

Amanda practically floated out of the tent. She knew she'd done the right thing.

But the devil still scolded her. "Don't you know the Bible says the person who doesn't provide for his own family is worse than a pagan who doesn't worship God?"

Amanda felt a stab of doubt. Had she done the wrong thing after all? But the peace of God continued to fill her heart. "I will just have to trust God for Maizie's shoes," she decided.

After a day of lively meetings, Amanda and Maizie were cutting up some peaches for their supper when a little boy ran up to them. "Grandpa says to come have supper with us in our tent!"

Maizie grinned. "Well, Ma, we better go. Brother Brummel won't let you say no."

Mother and daughter followed the little boy back to his family tent. Two extra plates had been set for the camp-style supper. Brother Brummel's eyes twinkled. "Sit here, Sister Smith!" he said, pointing to a place at the table. All the plates were turned upside down to keep the dust off.

After the prayer, Amanda turned her plate up. There, underneath, were three one-dollar bills—one more than she needed for Maizie's shoes.

"Praise the Lord!" she shouted—then laughed. The old devil sure got himself whipped that time!

*Trust is believing God will take care of you
even when He asks you to make a sacrifice for Him.*

FROM GOD'S WORD:

My God will use his wonderful riches in Christ Jesus to give you everything you need (Philippians 4:19).

LET'S TALK ABOUT IT:

1. Do you think Amanda Smith did the right thing giving two dollars to missions when her daughter needed shoes? Why or why not?
2. How did the devil try to discourage her?
3. In what ways does your family trust God to give you what you need, and in what ways do you rely on your own resources (money, job, etc.)?

Forgiveness

THE BEST WAY TO FIGHT

The special service at the Mayflower Mission in Brooklyn, New York, was over. Amanda Smith stepped down from the plain, wooden platform as a young man pushed through the crowd to speak to her. His handsome face was a dark cloud of gloom.

"Mrs. Smith," he said, clutching his hat, "I was deeply touched by what you said about God wanting us to forgive our enemies." The hat twisted in the man's hands. "I want to forgive my enemy, but . . . I just know it won't work."

Bit by bit, his story tumbled out. Charles Brown and another young man, Will Darcy, had been boyhood friends. When they grew up, they went into business and worked in the same office. Both were members of the Mayflower Mission Church. "But," said Charles, "several years ago, we had a quarrel. We both said harsh, unkind things, and now we haven't spoken to each other in four years. Oh, Mrs. Smith, each day that I see Will and he doesn't speak is an agony! I don't think I can stand it any longer. I'm thinking about leaving the church altogether. My wife begs me not to leave the church, but—"

"Why don't you go speak to him?" Amanda asked gently.

"I'm afraid if I do, he will curse me—and I just couldn't bear it."

"If you decide to do the right thing, God will help you," she encouraged. "Let's pray together right now, and you go talk to him tomorrow. Then tomorrow night, come back here to the mission and tell me what God has done."

The next day, as she got ready for the evening service, Amanda got down on her knees and prayed that this young man could experience the freedom of forgiveness. That evening as she spoke, she scanned the crowd. There sat Charles Brown—and his face was like a sunbeam. Right after the service, he came up to her quickly and said, "Oh, Mrs. Smith, praise the Lord! Everything is all right."

"I told you God would help you," she said. "What happened?"

Again the story tumbled out. All the way to work, Charles prayed he would have the courage to speak. Usually, he was the first to arrive, but that morning, Will was there before him and they were alone. "So I just blurted out, 'Look here, Will, I think it is time you and I were done with this foolishness of ours'—and do you know what he did, Mrs. Smith? He jumped to his feet, grabbed my hand, and with tears in his eyes said, 'I've been wanting to speak to you for a month, but I was afraid you wouldn't speak to me.' Both of us were afraid to be the first one to speak! Quickly, we asked forgiveness and forgave each other—and now we are old friends again."

Amanda's heart nearly burst with joy. If God did nothing else during these special services at the Mayflower Mission, it was worth it to have these two friends living in peace with each other. "You know, Mr. Brown," she said, a twinkle in her eye, "the devil would rather you settled your quarrel by fighting a duel. But the best way to fight a duel with an enemy is on your knees."

Forgiveness doesn't wait for your enemy to ask to be forgiven,
but finds the courage to speak first.

FROM GOD'S WORD:

Get along with each other, and forgive each other. If someone does wrong to you, forgive that person because the Lord forgave you (Colossians 3:13).

LET'S TALK ABOUT IT:

1. Why do you think it was so hard for the young man to speak to his old friend who had become his enemy?
2. What did Amanda Smith mean when she said, "The best way to fight a duel with an enemy is on your knees"?
3. Have you fought with someone lately and now find it hard to speak to that person? Ask God to give you courage to go speak to that person first and ask forgiveness.

CHARLES ALBERT TINDLEY

Prince of Preachers

In 1856, on a small farm outside Berlin, Maryland, a little boy was born to a slave couple, Ester and Charles Tindley. The little boy was also named Charles, but his mama died when he was two, and his daddy was unable to care for him. So Charles was "hired out" to other families and farmers to do chores.

Even though the Emancipation Proclamation freed all slaves in 1863, it made little difference to young Charles. His employers were harsh and did not permit him to go to school or church. But Charles had a curious mind. Finding scraps of newspaper along the roadway, he hid them inside his shirt and studied them late at night. Bit by bit he learned his ABC's and taught himself to read. The only book he had was the Bible, and he read it from cover to cover, skipping the words he couldn't figure out.

One day he slipped into a church, trying to hide his tattered clothes and bare feet by sitting in the balcony. But the preacher invited all boys and girls who could read the Bible to come up front to read. Charles sat up. He was a boy who could read the Bible! Ignoring the stares of the congregation, he marched up front and took his turn reading. Everyone was astounded. From that moment on, all Charles wanted to do was learn. He adopted a rule "to learn at least one new thing—a thing I did not know the day before—each day."

During the day, Charles worked as a "hod carrier," toting bricks, mortar, sand, and gravel for construction companies for $1.50 day. After work he went to night school, the "Institute for Colored Youths." He fell in love with Daisy Henry, a local girl, and married her. Hearing about the better opportunities for blacks in Philadelphia, the young couple moved to the big city and found a church home at John Wesley Methodist Episcopal Church (later called Bainbridge Street Methodist Episcopal). Eagerly, Charles agreed to be the church sexton, or janitor. This put him at the church almost daily, where he sat in on Bible classes, talked to the pastor, and read the pastor's books. Making a public confession of faith, he now knew what he wanted to be: a pastor and preacher.

He didn't let the fact that he had little formal education stop him. He studied Greek and Hebrew by mail and finally took the exam to be ordained as a pastor in 1885. After being sent to several other churches in New Jersey, Delaware, and Maryland, he accepted a call back to Bainbridge Street, his "home church," and became its pastor in 1901.

At six feet three, with a strong, low voice and powerful preaching style, Rev. Charles Albert Tindley became a powerful presence in Philadelphia and among Methodist churches. A frequent delegate to the annual and general conferences, he became known as "Mr. Delaware Conference." He built up his church from 130 members to 7,000 members and outgrew several buildings. The worship at his church—and churches everywhere—grew stronger by his over forty-five published gospel hymns. Toward the end of his life, he oversaw the construction of "a beautiful cathedral to give glory to God," which the Methodist conference named Tindley Temple as a way to honor his contributions. When he died in 1933 at the age of seventy-seven, Rev. Tindley had earned the reputation of "Prince of Preachers," by which he is still known today.

Hope

HEAVEN'S CHRISTMAS TREE

While pastoring a church in Wilmington, Delaware, Rev. Charles Tindley visited Philadelphia, his spiritual home. Here he had served as a janitor years before; here he had given his heart fully to the Lord; here he had dug into the Bible, read theology books, and taken correspondence courses (through the mail) in Greek and Hebrew; here he had been ordained as a pastor.

It was Christmas Day, and Rev. Tindley walked the quiet streets, thinking and praying. Passing a large church, he saw the doors open and people coming in and out. Curious, he came closer and through the open doors saw a large Christmas tree trimmed with colorful garlands. All over the tree, colorful packages were tied to the branches.

As he watched, a young man on a stepladder used a rod to lift a package from the tree. As he read the name on it aloud, an excited hand would shoot up from the pews. Rev. Tindley continued to watch until all the packages had been distributed. Boys and girls, men and women, happily passed out of the sanctuary, each with their gift.

And then Rev. Tindley saw a little boy, poorly dressed for how cold it was, one of the last to leave. His pinched face was trying to look brave, but his lip trembled. There had been no package with his name on the tree.

Oh, Father in heaven! Rev. Tindley's heart cried out. *Will there ever be a time when the spirit of Christ shall so fill and control the lives of people that everybody, young and old, rich and poor, will receive some token of love on Christmas Day?*

Almost in reply, a verse in Revelation came into his mind: "Then the angel showed me the river of the water of life. It was shining like crystal and was flowing from the throne of God and of the Lamb down the middle of the street of the city. The tree of life was on each side of the river" (Revelation 22:1–2). Suddenly, Tindley knew God had given him the answer. Jesus is the Tree of Life. He is "Heaven's Christmas Tree" come to earth on Christmas Day with wonderful gifts for every person on earth!

Several years later, Rev. Charles Tindley was back in Philadelphia pastoring the East Calvary Methodist Episcopal Church. At Christmastime he told his congregation the story about the little boy and how God had shown him that Jesus was "Heaven's Christmas Tree." "No one needs to go away empty-handed!" Rev. Tindley preached as he described the following gifts on the Tree of Life:

Hope for the Hopeless. This gift is on the lowest branches of the Tree of Life, within easy reach for everyone. It shines with all of God's promises to sinners and all those who feel discouraged by life's conflicts.

Forgiveness for the Guilty. This gift is the most costly gift, stained with the blood of Calvary. Every single person needs this gift, and there's enough for everyone.

Help for the Weak. Human nature cannot fight against the evils of this world—the temptations of the flesh, pride, and selfishness. But Jesus Christ is stronger than all the temptations of our worldly nature; He is our strength in the fight against evil.

Friendship for the Friendless. A person may be rich in the world's material goods but is poor without a friend. The human soul needs friends, but people often let us down. Jesus is the Friend who will always be there for us.

Peace far the Troubled Soul. God doesn't promise us a trouble-free life. What He does promise is a "peace that passes understanding" in spite of the troubles of life.

Home for the Homeless. Jesus has gone to heaven to prepare an eternal home for every single person who accepts Him as Savior. Regardless of our circumstances on earth, we have a home waiting for us, full of joy and glory.

After hearing Tindley's Christmas sermon, many people in the congregation came forward to receive these gifts from Jesus, the Tree of Life. Year after year, people came from far and wide at Christmastime to hear Rev. Charles Tindley's famous sermon, "Heaven's Christmas Tree." And many people went away with their names newly written in the Book of Life.

The hope we have in Jesus is a gift to be shared with others.

FROM GOD'S WORD:

Always be ready to answer everyone who asks you to explain about the hope you have (1 Peter 3:15).

LET'S TALK ABOUT IT:

1. Why do you think the little boy didn't have a gift with his name on it?
2. Rev. Tindley used everyday stories to tell about important spiritual truths in his sermons. Can you tell about an everyday event that reminded you about a spiritual truth?
3. Do you know someone who needs to know about the gifts from "Heaven's Christmas Tree"? How could you tell him or her about Jesus, the Tree of Life'?

Compassion

"NO CHARGE"

Rev. Charles Tindley pushed his way past the long line of out-of-work people lined up outside the local "soup kitchen." Times were hard in 1908, and black folks often felt the bite of poverty first as jobs disappeared. The city of Philadelphia responded by setting up bathhouses and soup kitchens in the poorer neighborhoods, but Tindley wanted to see for himself how the need was being met.

The soup was watery; the bread was stale. Rev. Tindley's heart went out to the dejected men, women, and children trying to survive on so little. If this was the best the city could—or would—do, the church ought to step forward.

The next Sunday morning he stood behind the pulpit at East Calvary Methodist Episcopal Church and came straight to the point. "In two weeks the members of this church are going to feed lunch to those without jobs and the hungry at our doorstep," he declared. "Jesus fed the multitudes, and He didn't charge them anything, either. If we are His followers, we must do the same."

The members of East Calvary willingly went to work. The auditorium below the sanctuary was turned into a daily soup kitchen. Local slaughterhouses donated chitterlings, pigs' ears, pigs' feet, gristly beef briskets, and occasional baskets of chickens. When cooked with kale, collard greens, or cabbage, they made a healthy, hot meal. Volunteers cooked, scrubbed floors, washed tablecloths, and helped raise money.

As the weather turned colder, some of the poor who came for lunch stayed till late in the afternoon, when they had to be sent away to make room for evening programs at the church—Bible classes, youth sings, prayer meetings. "It's cold out there, pastor," they said to Rev. Tindley. "We don't have any place to sleep."

Again Rev. Tindley talked to his members. Would they be willing to turn the auditorium into sleeping space for the homeless? It would mean giving up some of their evening programs or finding other places to meet. "Remember what it was like for you and me when we grew up in rural Delaware and Maryland," he reminded them. "We never let a neighbor go hungry or without a place to sleep. Just because we live in the city now, it should be no different. We need to take care of one another."

Many of East Calvary's members shared Rev. Tindley's compassion for the poor. But some of the more wealthy members didn't appreciate the lower-class folks who were beginning to attend church. They wanted to be like the elite congregations over at Cherry Street African Baptist or St. Thomas Episcopal. Rev. Tindley would have none of it. From the pulpit he plainly told these complainers that their attitude was unchristian. "Jesus didn't seek out the rich and powerful. He ministered to the poor, needy, and rejected." Some of the complainers left the church, but they were quickly replaced by new members from the streets.

But not all the "needy" came to East Calvary's soup kitchen. Two blocks away from the church was a strip of bars, gambling joints, and other "night life." Rev. Tindley often left his study and walked among the drunks, entertainers, gamblers, and prostitutes who strutted the streets. He pleaded with them to leave these sinful pursuits and come to the Cross. Although only a few responded, Rev. Tindley always came back to talk and express his concern. Many on the streets referred to him as "our pastor."

One day a man who was obviously drunk saw Rev. Tindley and greeted him loudly. "Rev. Tin'ley," he slurred. "I wanna shake your hand. You saved me."

Looking the man up and down, Tindley said wryly, "Yes, you look like the result of my work." He knew it was only the saving grace of Jesus who could save such men.

East Calvary's outreach to the poor was reported in one of the city's newspapers. One day the mayor showed up while lunch was being served. Seeing the hundreds being fed, the mayor took Rev. Tindley aside, pulled out his wallet, and gave him five hundred dollars for the work. "This is not a political move," he said. "I don't want one word of this in the newspapers. To profit from the circumstances of these poor folks would destroy any good that might be done. God bless your work."

Compassion is responding to people's needs in the same way Jesus did.

FROM GOD'S WORD:

When he [Jesus] saw the crowds, he felt sorry for them because they were hurting and helpless, like sheep without a shepherd (Matthew 9:36).

LET'S TALK ABOUT IT:

1. Why did Rev. Tindley think it was Christians' responsibility to feed hungry people?
2. Why did some church members complain?
3. How does your family or church help feed hungry people or provide shelter for the homeless?

Praise

THE SINGING PREACHER

Sometimes when Rev. Charles Albert Tindley was preaching about the faithfulness of God to his congregation in Philadelphia's East Calvary Methodist Episcopal Church, he would suddenly start to sing. Then he'd grin sheepishly. "Sorry. Couldn't help myself. Just a little song of mine that's been going around in my head lately."

"Pastor," some of the church members said to him, "you ought to write those songs down. Maybe you could even teach them to the choir to sing."

Music was an important part of worship at East Calvary. The choir and congregation sang a mix of great Methodist hymns and old Negro "slave" spirituals being made popular at that time by the Fisk (University) Jubilee Singers. Some of the older folks, like Rev. Tindley himself, had been born into slavery in the South. But even in the North, blacks struggled with second-class citizenship and prejudice. Many of their ordinary civil rights were still denied. Music was a way to express the deep pain and struggles of life and the saving grace of Jesus that helped them each day.

Tindley's first published hymn in 1901 was an evangelistic song based on the story of Naaman the leper: "Go Wash in the Beautiful Stream."

By 1909, he had published over twenty gospel hymns, such as "Stand By Me" and "Nothing Between My Soul and the Savior."

Three of Tindley's eight children inherited his musical gifts, as well. Emmaline, the middle daughter, broke her father's heart when she had a child out of marriage; but Tindley received his prodigal daughter back home and raised the child as one of the family. Emmaline had a beautiful soprano voice and became a gifted soloist with the East Calvary choir. Her specialty was singing her father's hymns. (She later married a young minister.) Tindley's oldest son, Frederick, a postal worker, could play the alto, bass, and baritone horns, as well as violin and trumpet; he organized an outstanding orchestra at East Calvary. Elbert, the youngest Tindley, was a poor student and a goof-off, but eventually he settled down, using his fine tenor voice as part of the choir and in duets with Emmaline.

Like many other songwriters, Tindley's hymns grew out of personal experiences that flowed out in music. In 1916, he was nominated for bishop in the Methodist General Conference but was not elected. Two more times he was nominated for bishop, but some of his "enemies" were determined that a self-taught former slave without a formal education should not represent black Methodism alongside the white bishops. He was defeated. One of his hymns contains the words, "I often wonder why it is / While some are happy and free / That I am tried and sore oppressed / But it may be the best for me.... The Lord knows the way / And I will obey / It may be the best for me." Even in his disappointment, he expressed his faith in the Lord.

One of Rev. Tindley's sons, Sergeant John Tindley, was killed in Europe during World War I. The pastor's grief was poured out in the hymn "I'll Be Satisfied," published in 1919 and dedicated to the memory of his son.

Tindley's associate pastor, Andrew Sellars, organized a men's Bible class at East Calvary. Out of this class, ten men and a pianist specialized in singing Rev. Tindley's gospel hymns in close harmony and became nationally known as the Tindley Gospel Singers. Thomas A. Dorsey, a popular gospel singer and songwriter, credited Charles Tindley with being his inspiration.

But Rev. Tindley did not write music to become famous. He wrote music to express the spiritual truths that helped him endure in his life—a life that began in slavery, was dedicated to sharing the good news of salvation, and was poured out in service and friendship to rich and poor, white and black alike.

Praise to the Lord is often expressed through music.

FROM GOD'S WORD:

Praise the Lord! Sing a new song to the Lord; sing his praise in the meeting of his people (Psalm 149:1).

LET'S TALK ABOUT IT:

1. Do you have any hymns written by Charles Albert Tindley in your church hymnal? Learn to sing one if it's not familiar to you.
2. Not everyone can write music like Rev. Tindley. Name all the different ways people can praise God through music.
3. Read Psalm 150, which could be titled: "Praise the Lord With Music." Choose one of the ways mentioned in this psalm to praise the Lord.

GEORGE WASHINGTON CARVER

The Man Who Saved the South From Poverty

In the fall of 1861, bushwhackers kidnapped a slave girl and her baby from a small Missouri farm, intending to resell them in the South. But Moses Carver, who had bought the girl as a companion for his wife, offered a $300 racehorse for their return. A bounty hunter went after them, but all he had to show for his efforts when he returned was the sickly infant. Carver gave him the racehorse anyway.

The lad was called George, and when the Emancipation Proclamation freed all slaves, he was raised as a member of the Carver family. Too frail for heavy farm work, he developed a deep love for all growing things. He also had a great desire to learn: Why did the roses grow here but not there? Why did the field crops produce less this year than the year before? He desperately wanted to learn to read, but the local white school wouldn't enroll colored children.

Determined to get an education, he left home at age fourteen, working odd jobs to support himself and going to school anywhere that would take him. George Carver wasted little time on bitterness even though racism threw cruel obstacles in his path again and again. Later in life he said, "If I used my energy to right every wrong done to me, I would have no energy left for my work." Eventually he received his master's degree in agriculture and bacterial botany from Iowa State College of Agriculture and Mechanic Arts, and two honorary doctorates.

Carver's thirst to understand God's created world knew no bounds. But why had God given him the skills to unlock nature's secrets? In 1896 he received a letter from Booker T. Washington from Tuskegee Institute in Alabama: Would he come and teach his people how to grow food? The only thing most Southerners knew how to grow was cotton—"King Cotton" they called it. But each year the cotton fields produced less and less. Add years of slavery, the ravages of the Civil War, and the injustices of racism, and most black Americans lived in grinding poverty. Suddenly he knew: God had revealed His plan for George Carver.

For the rest of his life, Dr. Carver dedicated his knowledge of science to helping the common man make a living. He developed two hundred new products from the peanut and 118 practical products from the sweet potato. In so doing, he broke King Cotton's grip on the South, renewing the tired soil and benefiting whites and blacks alike.

The humblest of men, he turned down many well-paying job offers and refused to take a raise in salary. When he died in 1943, he was still receiving the same $125 a week he had started with over forty years earlier. His epitaph reads: "He could have added fortune to fame, but caring for neither, he found happiness and honor in helping the world."

Perseverance

"BE LIKE LIBBY"

George Carver's eyes widened as he untied the paper wrapping and took out the worn brown leather Bible. "A Christmas present for me?" he said in surprise.

"For when you learn to read," said the kindly midwife. Mariah Watkins had seen the fourteen-year-old boy sitting on her fence earlier that fall of 1875, looking hungry and lost. He'd walked to Neosha, Missouri, to attend the Lincoln School for Colored Children, but he had no money or a place to live. The Watkinses had taken him in and were amazed at how hard he worked for his keep. This boy had promise.

"Do you know how to read, Aunt Mariah?" George asked.

Mariah's eyes got misty. "Before the Civil War, I was a slave, just like your mammy. Of all the slaves on the plantation, only one, a woman named Libby, knew how to read. If our master had found out, she probably would've been sold downriver to the South quick as a blink because any slave who had some learnin' was considered uppity and dangerous. But Libby refused to keep this gift to herself and secretly taught some of the rest of us how to read." Mariah took the boy by the shoulders. "George, you must learn all you can, then be like Libby. Go out in the world and give your learnin' back to our people. They're starvin' for a little learnin'."

George was eager to learn and began reading the Bible—a daily habit that gave him strength to the end of his life. But he soon learned everything the Neosha teacher could teach him. Hitching a wagon ride to Fort Scott, Kansas, he got a job cooking to earn money for school books. But one day he saw a colored man dragged out of a jail and burned to death by an angry mob. Frightened, he realized it was dangerous to have dark skin in Fort Scott.

Traveling from town to town in the Midwest, doing odd jobs, George finally graduated from high school. He excelled in botany, biology, chemistry, and art—but there was so much more to learn! Hardly daring to hope, he applied to a Presbyterian college in Highland, Kansas. One day the longed-for letter arrived: He had been accepted! That fall he eagerly arrived on campus. But the dean took one look and said, "You didn't tell us you were a Negro. Highland College does not take Negroes."

George was devastated. Was this the end of the road?

A few years later, renewing his courage, he applied to Simpson College and was accepted—only the second black person in the college's history. At his art teacher's urging, he transferred to the Iowa State College of Agriculture and Mechanic Arts to study horticulture—even though he was barred from the student dining room and had to eat with the kitchen staff. He suffered this indignity patiently, telling himself that ignorant people would not keep him from his duty. The school quickly changed its mind when a prominent white woman who admired George's paintings came to visit him and insisted on eating with him in the kitchen.

After obtaining his master's degree, George was offered a job as professor at Iowa State. But in his mind he heard Mariah Watkins' voice saying, "Be like Libby. Give your learnin' back to your people." When a letter from Tuskegee Institute in Alabama arrived, asking Professor Carver to come teach southern blacks new ways to farm, he knew immediately this was the task God had been preparing him for all along.

Perseverance is knowing God's love is more powerful than the obstacles evil people put in our way.

FROM GOD'S WORD:

Can anything separate us from the love Christ has for us? Can troubles or problems or sufferings or hunger or nakedness or danger or violent death? . . . In all these things we have full victory through God who showed his love for us (Romans 8:35, 37).

LET'S TALK ABOUT IT:

1. What were the obstacles George faced that would have made the average person give up the idea of getting an education?
2. How do you think George had the courage to overcome the racism he faced again and again?
3. What obstacles in your life are keeping you from a God-given goal?

Resourcefulness

MOST WEEDS HAVE A PURPOSE

I cannot offer you money, position, or fame," Booker T. Washington had written to George Carver. "I offer you in their place work—hard, hard work—the task of bringing a people from degradation, poverty, and waste to full personhood."

As Dr. Carver, satchel in hand, stood looking at the dreary frame buildings and barren, dusty grounds of the Tuskegee Institute, Washington's words took on grim meaning. The soil was starving, drained of its nutrients by centuries of planting only cotton. But some things were growing here and there. Curiously, Carver set down his bag and began picking this leafy stalk, then that one, until he had an armful.

"Lad," he called to the boy who had picked him up from the train, "what is the name of this plant?"

"That?" said the boy. "It's a weed."

"They're all weeds." Carver smiled. "But every weed has a name, and most of them have a purpose."

Within a few weeks, Professor Carver had thirteen students and a task: to set up a laboratory to test local soil and find ways to enrich it for farming. Only one hitch; there was no money to buy equipment for a laboratory.

Carver had never let the lack of money stand in his way. God had given him a brain, and he intended to use it. Marching his students to the school dump, he directed them to save everything possible: bottles, cooking pots, jar lids, wire, odd bits of metal, rusty lamps, broken handles. When the dump had been thoroughly searched, they scoured the back alleys of Tuskegee for china dishes, rubber, curtain rods, and flatirons.

"All this may seem to be just junk to you," he told his skeptical students. "But it is only waiting for us to apply our intelligence to it. Let's get to work!"

Under Carver's supervision, the students punched holes in pieces of tin to make strainers to test soil samples; neatly labeled canning jars held an assortment of chemicals; broken bottles were cut down and transformed into beakers; a discarded ink bottle with a cork and a piece of string made do nicely as a Bunsen burner.

Gradually the makeshift laboratory took shape. And a valuable lesson was learned by the Tuskegee students that carried over into later years, when they took their knowledge into the poverty-stricken pockets of the South. Expensive or brand-new equipment was not a requirement for success.

Dr. Carver was never satisfied with only the obvious use of a thing, especially when it came to things in nature. He firmly believed God had provided all that people needed in the created world; God left it to humans to figure out the secrets locked within each plant, animal, or mineral. To many, a peanut was just a snack and not worth growing as a crop. But with Dr. Carver's probing curiosity and scientific knowledge, the peanut produced butter, oil, milk, dye, salve, shaving cream, paper, shampoo, metal polish, stains, adhesives, plastics, wallboard, and more—for a total of three hundred products! It was this variation that provided new markets for southern crops and saved the South from ruin.

Resourcefulness is using our God-given minds to see usefulness in things (or people) that others just throw away.

FROM GOD'S WORD:

My God will use his wonderful riches in Christ Jesus to give you everything you need (Philippians 4:19).

LET'S TALK ABOUT IT:

1. Why do you think Dr. Carver learned to be resourceful?
2. How is resourcefulness a way of being a good steward of God's creation?
3. Look at some things you throw away. How might you make them useful again?

Service

THE SCHOOL ON WHEELS

Dr. George Washington Carver bent down and cut a huge head of cabbage, then lifted it for the openmouthed farmers crowded around him. "These were the worst twenty acres in Alabama four years ago," he said dryly. "Now each acre is producing a $75 profit."

It was Farmers' Institute Day at Tuskegee Institute. On the third Tuesday of each month, Dr. Carver talked to local farmers about the importance of rotating their crops and how rotted leaves and kitchen wastes could enrich their soil. "Don't burn off your corn stalks," he scolded. "That's like burning off the outside bills on a roll of dollars. Plow them back into the soil. It's free fertilizer."

As the farmers left, shaking their heads in amazement, Tom Campbell, one of Carver's students, grinned. "Soon as their neighbors see those farmers growing bigger melons than they are, every farmer in Macon County will be hoofin' it up here on third Tuesdays to see your experiment station."

Dr. Carver rubbed his chin thoughtfully. For months he'd been thinking about the dirt-poor farmers tucked away in little hollows all over the county. "No, Tom," he said, "if we want to help the man farthest down take a step up, we're going to have to take the school to them. Say . . . do you think you could scare up a wagon and a horse?"

So it was that the "school man" from Tuskegee and Tom Campbell could be seen each weekend driving the back roads that fall of 1899. It wasn't easy persuading farmers to try something new. "What makes you think you smarter'n me?" scoffed one. "You just as black." Out would come sample plants, and Dr. Carver would patiently explain how they could plant two crops of sweet potatoes a year and feed their hogs with the vines, culls, and peelings—and still do less damage to the soil than one crop of cotton.

"Each plant takes certain things from the soil," he explained. "If you plant only one thing year after year, the soil is soon drained. But chickpeas take nitrogen from the air and put it back into the soil."

"Chickpeas!" snorted a housewife. "What good are chickpeas?" Then Dr. Carver would roll up his sleeves, put a pot of chickpeas on the wood-burning stove, and turn out a tasty meal with mashed chickpeas as the main ingredient in three or four dishes.

Some of Carver's students were doubtful of the school on wheels. "That's no way to make money—giving away free advice."

Carver's eyes flashed fire. "I'm not here to contribute to your own gain," he said, "but to help you lead your people forward. That will be the mark of your success, not the style of clothes you wear, nor the amount of money you put in the bank. It is only service that counts!"

In fact, Carver considered the school on wheels his most important work. He taught backwoods people medical remedies from herbs and plants, how to brighten up their buildings with paints made from color-rich dirt, how to dry fruits and vegetables to feed their families all year long.

And the idea spread. Soon lots of wagons were traveling the back roads. In 1918, the state of Alabama provided a huge motorized truck for the traveling school. Other schools began copying the idea. Educators from foreign countries visited Tuskegee Institute to ask how they could adapt Carver's idea.

When Dr. Carver died in 1943, the chaplain of the school said, "He worshiped God by drawing out of the things that grow goodnesses to serve the needs of mankind."

Service is using God's gifts for the good of others, not for our own gain.

FROM GOD'S WORD:

Each of you has received a gift to use to serve others. Be good servants of God's various gifts of grace (1 Peter 4:10).

LET'S TALK ABOUT IT:

1. Dr. Carver was a brilliant scientist. He also suffered from prejudice and poverty. Think of several ways he could have become a very rich man.
2. Why do you think he chose to use his gifts to serve other people instead?
3. What gifts do you have (skills, knowledge, etc.) that could lead to "success" in the world? How might you use those gifts serving others?

WILLIAM J. SEYMOUR

"Father" of Modern Pentecostals

When William Seymour was a boy, he often imagined seeing God. He was born on May 2, 1870, in Centerville, Louisiana, to Simon and Phyllis Seymour, former slaves, who raised him as a Baptist. But Sunday school wasn't enough. William studied the Bible on his own to check out whether his visions of God were true.

At the age of twenty-five, William moved to Indianapolis, where he worked as a railroad porter and a waiter in a fashionable restaurant and attended a black Methodist Episcopal church.

In 1900 he moved to Cincinnati, Ohio, and enrolled in a holiness Bible school. There he studied sanctification (how God makes us holy), healing, and the expectation that there would be a worldwide revival in the Holy Spirit before the Lord's soon return.

Seymour heard God call him to become a preacher, but he resisted until he caught smallpox, an often deadly disease. William recovered but lost the sight in one eye due to infection. Having been so sick, he realized that one should be quick to obey God's call. So he immediately accepted ordination as a preacher.

One day William Seymour received a letter from a small church in Los Angeles. One of its members had heard Seymour preach, and the church invited him to be their pastor. A train ticket was included in the letter.

At the new church in Southern California, Seymour preached that the Holy Spirit (or Holy Ghost, as He was often called) was eager to baptize every believer with power just like what was reported in the book of Acts. After a month of intense prayer and fasting, in April 1906 the Holy Spirit fell in power on the small group, and several members spoke in tongues. The experience was like fire, spreading so quickly that huge crowds began coming every day and every night to the mission at 312 Azusa Street. People were healed of sickness, hundreds were converted to Christ, and many were sent out as missionaries around the world. (See the TRAILBLAZER BOOK *Journey to the End of the Earth.*)

This powerful move of the Spirit became known as the Azusa Street Revival. Within two years, the movement took root in over fifty nations. Today, the spiritual heirs of the Azusa Street Revival number over half a billion people, making Pentecostals and Charismatics (as they are often called) the second largest and the fastest-growing family of Christians in the world. It includes the Church of God in Christ, the Assemblies of God, Apostolic Church, Four Square Church of God, and numerous other denominations and independent "full Gospel" churches. Whether black or white, Hispanic or Asian, almost all churches in this movement can trace their roots directly or indirectly to the humble mission at 312 Azusa Street and its pastor, William J. Seymour.

Discernment

THE HEADLESS PHANTOM

Hurrying home alone one night, young Willie Seymour thought he would save a little time by taking a shortcut . . . through a cemetery. The boy stepped through a hole in the fence but found it hard to see any distinct path. In the dark he weaved his way between the gravestones, trying not to trip over low ones that might be hidden in the grass.

He had just come around a tree when he noticed a shape a short distance ahead of him. Unlike the tall gravestones that appeared a bluish gray in the moonless night, this shape was dark and about as tall as a man.

Willie stopped and steadied himself with his hand on the tree to his side.

Suddenly he thought he saw the shape move. He blinked. Maybe his eyes were playing tricks on him as they tried to recognize something familiar in the darkness.

A second time the shape seemed to move. Willie blinked again, and this time stepped a little closer to the tree, thinking he might hide behind it. But the dark shape held steady. The harder he stared, the less he could see until the shadow seemed to disappear altogether. Then it moved again . . . and this time there was no mistake. It was moving, and it was coming toward him.

Soon he could even make out its feet, taking one step at a time. He could see its body and shoulders as though they were wrapped in a great coat. But . . . there was no head!

It looked like a headless man walking right toward him!

Willie's heart pounded harder and harder as he tried to tell himself that there was no such thing as a walking headless man, and yet, at that moment, he was watching one coming his way. Every nerve in his body wanted to flee, and yet he held his ground. He did not believe in ghosts and phantoms, and so he was not going to run away from something just because it looked like one.

But *something* was coming toward him. In fact, while blinking his eyes and hoping it would disappear, he heard the specter's feet crunching on dry grass and twigs. Not only his eyes but now his ears told him something was coming.

And then, when the phantom was no more than a few yards away, it raised its head . . . and he saw with great relief that it was not a headless man but an old horse that had simply been grazing its way through the cemetery with its head to the ground.

That old horse did not fool young Willie Seymour, and years later when magicians and con artists tried to fake God's miracles, Seymour was not easily fooled.

It seems like every time God does a great work by His Spirit, con artists try to gain fame and take people's money by performing a counterfeit. Frank Bartleman, one of the white leaders who assisted William Seymour, wrote, "We had the most to fear from the working of evil spirits within. Even spiritualists and hypnotists came to investigate and to try their influence. Then all the religious soreheads and crooks and cranks came seeking a place in the work. We had the most to fear from these."

Pastor Seymour wisely and quietly "prayed" these trouble causers into silence. He knew that if he drew too much attention to the devil's activities, the people would become afraid. They might fear that their free forms of worship and their exercise of spiritual gifts did not come from the Holy Spirit but from some evil spirit.

Bartleman claims that many times when someone got up to disrupt the meetings, "Their minds would wander, their brains reeling. Things would turn black before their eyes. They could not go on. I never saw one get by with it in those days. They were up against God. No one cut them off. We simply prayed. The Holy Spirit did the rest."

Discernment provides wisdom and safety in frightening circumstances.

FROM GOD'S WORD:

Do not fear anything except the Lord Almighty. He alone is the Holy One. If you fear him, you need fear nothing else (Isaiah 8:13 NLT).

LET'S TALK ABOUT IT:

1. Why didn't William Seymour run when he thought he saw a headless man walking toward him?
2. Tell about a time when you were scared in the dark. What did you do?
3. How can fear cloud our judgment (discernment)? Think about the Bible verse from Isaiah 8:13. Why do we not need to fear anything other than God?

Reconciliation

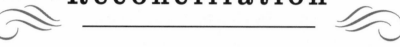

WASHING AWAY THE COLOR LINE

No! I won't allow a colored man in my classroom," said the teacher when William Seymour asked to attend his Bible school in Houston, Texas. "It's just not right to mix the races."

"But how can I learn about the Holy Spirit?" asked Seymour. "If what you say about a coming revival is true, I don't want to miss out."

"Well . . . well, you can sit outside the door in the hallway. Maybe you can hear a little there."

So that's how William Seymour attended Charles F. Parham's Bible school in 1905. Seymour had come to Houston a couple of years earlier to look for some relatives his family had lost track of during slavery. When he found them, they invited him to live with them while he preached at various churches in the area.

One day he met a young black woman, Lucy Farrow, who worked as a governess for the Parham family. Parham traveled around the Midwest preaching, evangelizing, and running short-term Bible schools. "When we were in Topeka, Kansas," Miss Farrow said, "a woman named Agnes Ozman spoke in unknown tongues, and then I did, too. Brother Parham says this is the first evidence of a Pentecostal revival. You ought to attend his Bible school here in Houston. It could change your life and your preaching forever."

So, in spite of the disgrace of being banished to the hallway, Seymour sat and listened. Parham said that in the last days God would pour out His Holy Spirit with power similar to what happened at Pentecost in the book of Acts. Believers would speak in tongues, prophesy, heal the sick, and spread the Gospel as never before. Parham had not yet experienced this renewal himself, but he believed that it was coming. After studying the Bible for himself, Seymour agreed and began preaching the same thing.

He took this message with him when he moved to Los Angeles to serve as pastor of a small mission there, and after a month of "waiting" in prayer and Bible study, the little congregation was "filled with the Holy Ghost, and began to speak with other tongues," similar to what was described in Acts 2:4.

But Seymour did not accept racial separation. He believed that the real miracle on the Day of Pentecost was the Holy Spirit's outpouring of so much godly love that three thousand people from "every nation under heaven" accepted the Gospel. The unity Jesus prayed for in John 17 was dramatically realized between former enemies and strangers. To Seymour, the gift of tongues was a way of communicating that love. And so the love that could unite people—blacks and whites, people from India and China and South America—was what mattered. Jesus shed His blood to forgive our sins and to wash away all divisions, including the "color line."

Six months later Charles Parham came to visit the Azusa Street Mission, apparently intending to take over. In his first message, he declared, "God is sick to His stomach" at all the racial mixing. Later his wife explained, "In Texas, you know, the colored people are not allowed to mix with the white people." Parham was a full-fledged racist and later became an open supporter of the Ku Klux Klan. He drew away some white people to start a rival church, as did other white leaders over the years until the Pentecostal movement became largely divided into black and white denominations.

However, many years later in 1994 and again in 1997, leaders of the Pentecostal and Charismatic Churches of North America (PCCNA) pursued reconciliation. After repenting and exchanging apologies and forgiveness, white and black leaders from the Assemblies of God, the Church of God in Christ, the Church of God of Prophecy, and various independent Pentecostal and charismatic groups washed one another's feet and pledged to eliminate racism in their churches.

Racial reconciliation helps fulfill Jesus' prayer in John 17:11 that we all be made one.

FROM GOD'S WORD:

Christ . . . made [all races] one people. They were separated as if there were a wall between them, but Christ broke down that wall of hate by giving his own body (Ephesians 2:14).

LET'S TALK ABOUT IT:

1. What do you think Charles Parham feared if he let black people sit with whites in his classroom?
2. Which two people should be closer to each other, a black Christian and a white Christian, or two relatives of the same race where one is a Christian and one is not?
3. Since Jesus prayed that we would all be made one, how can you obey His will when you meet a Christian from another race?

Faithfulness

MANY LANGUAGES,
MANY GIFTS, ONE GOSPEL

On the day Christians were first baptized by the Holy Spirit, we are told in Acts 2 that three thousand people believed. Many of these were foreigners who heard the Christians speaking in "tongues"—their own language. Later in the New Testament it appears that speaking in tongues served other purposes as well, such as praising God (Acts 10:46) or prophesying (1 Corinthians 14:6).

At William Seymour's Azusa Street Mission, spreading the Gospel was just as important as it was to the first Christians, and just like the New Testament believers, they sometimes used their gift of tongues to do it.

Sister Anna Hall visited a Russian church in Los Angeles and, by the power of the Holy Spirit, spoke to them in their own language. They were so glad that they wept and kissed her hand. They visited the Azusa Mission a few nights later when Brother Lee was empowered by the Spirit to speak and sing in their language. The Holy Spirit then fell on the Russian believers, and they, too, began glorifying God.

On August 10, 1906, on their way to Jerusalem as missionaries, Andrew Johnson, Louise Condit, and Lucy Leatherman stopped in Oakland,

California. They had been selected as missionaries because they had received several Middle Eastern languages. While in Oakland they were talking on the street about the gift of tongues, when Lucy Leatherman began speaking in tongues just as a man wearing a Turkish fez came by. He stopped and listened and then said in English, "You obviously are American, but in what university did you learn Turkish?"

When she explained that it was a gift from God, he was amazed. "I am from the university in Constantinople, but yours is the most perfect Turkish I have heard spoken by a foreigner."

She laughed and said, "Then you may not understand why I do not know what I have just said. Could you interpret for me?"

He did, and they continued speaking about the Gospel of Jesus Christ.

Some time later Lucy Farrow went on a short-term mission to West Africa and was enabled by the Holy Spirit to preach two sermons in the Kru language to the residents of Johnsonville, twenty-five miles south of Monrovia. Many accepted Christ and received the Holy Spirit, speaking in other tongues, some in English that Miss Farrow could understand perfectly.

Similar experiences followed dozens of missionaries from the Azusa Street Mission, who were sent all over the world—to India, China, Africa, Japan, Sweden, Ireland, Egypt, Palestine, and elsewhere. However, the ability to speak in a *specific* foreign tongue did not seem to be a permanent gift for most missionaries. "Tongues" became more and more an expression of prayer and praise and prophecy as we see happened in the latter portion of the New Testament.

Why wasn't it a permanent gift for these missionaries? Possibly the Lord used that particular gift to get the missionaries on the field and to get the work started. But then most had to buckle down to the hard task of learning the language of the people in order to carry on the work.

No matter what spiritual gift God gives us, we should use it faithfully.

*Faithfulness helps us use spiritual gifts in a way
that builds up the church and spreads the Gospel.*

FROM GOD'S WORD:

God has given gifts to each of you from his great variety of spiritual gifts. Manage them well so that God's generosity can flow through you (1 Peter 4:10 NLT).

LET'S TALK ABOUT IT:

1. What was the purpose behind speaking in tongues and the use of other spiritual gifts at the Asuza Street Mission?
2. Why do you think the Russian-Americans responded so gladly when they heard someone from the Azusa Street Mission sharing the Gospel in Russian?
3. Make a list of all the "spiritual gifts" you can find in the New Testament (1 Corinthians 12:4-11; Ephesians 4:11). What spiritual gift(s) has God given you? How can you use your gift faithfully?

MARY McLEOD BETHUNE

Teacher of Head, Hands, and Heart

Sam and Patsy McLeod and ten of their children were born into slavery on a cotton plantation in Mayesville, South Carolina. But the Emancipation Proclamation of 1863 ended five generations of slavery for the McLeod family, and their fifteenth child, Mary Jane, who came into the world on July 10, 1875, was born free.

But "born free" for blacks in the South didn't necessarily mean "equal." As Mary struggled to understand her world, she decided the main difference between white people and black people was that white people could read. To go to school became her burning passion. When a school for black children was finally started in Mayesville, eleven-year-old Mary became an eager student.

Within a few years, the teacher recommended her for a scholarship to Scotia Seminary in Concord, North Carolina—a school for the daughters of "freedmen"—where Mary studied literature, Greek, Latin, the Bible, and American democracy. She soaked up knowledge like a thirsty sponge, but she also wanted to give back what she learned. Deciding to become a missionary to her own people back in Africa, she attended Moody Bible Institute in Chicago. But when she graduated and applied to the Presbyterian Mission Board, she was told, "We have no openings for a colored missionary in Africa."

It was the bitterest disappointment of Mary's life. But it was also a turning point. If she couldn't go to Africa, she would teach her people right here at home in the South.

While teaching at Kendell Institute in Sumter, Georgia, she met a handsome young teacher named Albertus Bethune, whom she married in 1898. A year later Albertus Jr. was born.

But Mary's dream of "giving back" deepened. She was glad for the black colleges that were being formed at the turn of the century, but what good was a college when so many black children in the South couldn't even read? In her mind was a school where young girls and boys would not only learn useful trades, but the arts and sciences and the rights and responsibilities of citizenship. "Greek and a toothbrush!" she'd laugh when someone asked about her beliefs on education.

Wealthy whites were going south to Florida during the harsh northern winters. This meant jobs for blacks working on the new railroad and putting up the new hotels. Shantytowns grew up for these workers near resort towns like Daytona Beach. This became Mary McLeod Bethune's mission field. She determined to build a school to teach the head (classical education), hands (practical education), and heart (spiritual education). In 1904 she started with five little girls . . . and by 1923, her vision had become Bethune-Cookman College in Daytona, Florida.

When Mrs. Bethune died in 1955, she had not only served as an inspiration to thousands of young black people but also as an advisor to President Franklin D. Roosevelt. She worked tirelessly for the Urban League, the NAACP, the National Council of Negro Women, the National Youth Administration, and the Federal Council of Negro Affairs. In her will she stated: "I leave you love . . . I leave you hope . . . I leave you a thirst for education . . . I leave, finally, a responsibility to our young people."

Faith

"BUT . . . WHERE'S THE SCHOOL?"

Thirteen-year-old Mary McLeod stood wide-eyed and open-mouthed, bag in hand, at the gate of Scotia Seminary for the Daughters of Freedmen (former slaves) in Concord, North Carolina. She had never imagined such a wonderful place. Brick buildings with white pillars stood among tree-shaded lawns. Surely someone would pinch her and tell her it was all a mistake. She didn't belong here.

Then she remembered. A Quaker woman out in Colorado had offered a scholarship to a Negro girl who would "make good," and Mary's teacher, Miss Wilson, had recommended Mary. She had been praying day and night for the chance to get an education. And now here she was. "Victory through faith!"

Mary threw herself into her studies: Greek, Latin, literature, Bible, and American democracy. When she finished the high school course, she took Scotia's Normal course to become a teacher herself. She wanted to give back everything she'd learned—and someday she'd have a school of her own, a school like Scotia. Except she would take her school to where the children were, the children who lived in the little shantytowns and back roads of the South, who didn't know how to read.

After graduation from Scotia, Mary accepted several teaching assignments in the South. But she was frustrated at the limited education black children were being offered. In her mind, her dream school began to grow.

1. She'd fill it with song to express the longings of her people.
2. It would look like Scotia, with beautiful buildings and grounds.
3. It would train boys and girls to work for a living, learning all sorts of skills and trades.
4. It would give all the world's learning, including the arts and sciences.
5. It would teach the duties and privileges of citizenship.
6. It would be a living part of the community—reaching out in service, building up her people to take their rightful place as productive citizens.

While teaching in Palatka, Florida, with her husband, Albertus, and little boy, Albert Jr., Mary noticed that many black families were following the new railroad down the leg of Florida, hoping for jobs. Shantytowns of railroad workers and hotel workers were growing up alongside wealthy winter resorts such as Daytona Beach. But who was going to teach their children?

With only $1.50 to her name, Mary and her little family set out for Daytona. Now she had a goal. Now she had a destination. This was where she would begin her school. "Victory through faith!" she told herself.

Starting with just five little girls and a four-room house that she rented for eleven dollars a month, Mrs. Bethune named her school "The Daytona Educational and Industrial Institute for Girls." As more and more girls came, the little house quickly became too small. She needed land. She needed to build. But where would she get the money?

Nothing, Mary Bethune reminded herself, was ever accomplished without acting in faith. Forming the girls into a choir, she began taking them to churches and hotels as a way to advertise the school and raise money. At one hotel, she met a distinguished gentleman with white hair who seemed genuinely interested in her description of the school. Happily, Mrs. Bethune invited him to come for a visit.

A few days later, a sleek black car drove up in front of the shabby little house. The white-haired gentleman got out and looked around. With curious girls crowding at the windows, Mrs. Bethune went out to meet him.

"But . . . where's the school?" he said, bewildered.

Mrs. Bethune smiled broadly. "In my mind and in my heart, Mr. Gamble! What you see is just the seed, which will soon grow. But we need a board of trustees, with men like you who also have a vision for what the school can become. Mr. Gamble, will you become our first trustee?"

Now Mr. Gamble was smiling, too. "I like your attitude, Mrs. Bethune," he said. "I would be honored to be the first trustee of your school."

Mr. Gamble—of Proctor and Gamble—became a valuable friend of Mary McLeod Bethune's school, and the first building to be built was named "Faith Hall."

Faith is claiming victory and acting on what you believe God wants you to do.

FROM GOD'S WORD:

Everyone who is a child of God conquers the world. And this is the victory that conquers the world—our faith (1 John 5:4).

LET'S TALK ABOUT IT:

1. What was Mrs. Bethune's way of "giving back" what she'd been given?
2. Why do you think Mrs. Bethune's motto became "Victory through faith"?
3. What is the difference between "having faith" and "acting in faith"?

Diligence

NO SUCH THING AS A MENIAL TASK

Welcome, girls!" Mary McLeod Bethune faced her first class of girls, her broad, dark face beaming. "Enter these doors to learn. Depart to serve."

The little school in a rented house on the edge of a shantytown in Daytona, Florida, didn't look like much. They had no school supplies and few books. Mrs. Bethune had no money, and some of the girls couldn't pay the fifty cents per week tuition. But the lack of money and supplies didn't stop Mrs. Bethune. Organizing the girls into scavenger teams, they combed the alleys and town dump for useable items like cooking pots and pounded the dents out of them. A packing box served as a desk. Charcoal splinters were used as pencils. Spanish moss hanging from the big oak trees was stuffed into cotton ticks for mattresses. Old clothes were made over to fit the girls.

Mornings were given to book studies: literature, Bible, Latin, history. Afternoons found the girls doing housekeeping chores and learning practical skills, such as how to bake pies, set a proper table, tend a garden, and sew up curtains for the windows. "We seek to educate the head, the hands, and the heart," Mrs. Bethune gently reminded the girls when they complained about having to scrub the floors again.

But not everyone was happy with Mrs. Bethune's philosophy of education. Some of her critics were black people like herself. "You're teaching the girls to do menial (lowly) work!" they fussed. "We don't want to be servants and laborers anymore! Our children need philosophy and science and the arts!"

"They need both," she countered. "Yes, our people need to reach for their fullest potential, but in the meantime, they need to make a living and take advantage of whatever opportunities are open to them. Besides," she huffed, "there is no such thing as menial work—only a menial attitude."

The Daytona Educational and Industrial Institute grew from five girls to twenty to two hundred . . . and more. Even though Mrs. Bethune went knocking on the doors of blacks and whites alike seeking support for the school, she and the girls worked hard to support themselves. They planted a vegetable garden and grew beans, carrots, sugarcane, strawberries, and sweet potatoes. Besides food for their own table, they sold fresh vegetables to the local tourists. The girls made sweet potato pies and sold them to the hungry railroad workers eager for some home cooking. Some of the older girls hired themselves out as helpers in wealthy white homes as a way to support themselves while getting an education.

"Oh, Mrs. Bethune," they wailed one day. "How will we ever get these clean?" They showed her a pile of fine white linen tablecloths.

"Boil them," she instructed.

The girls looked at one another. Boil them? That meant making a fire out in the yard and waiting while the big tub of water heated up. So much work!

Later in the day, Mrs. Bethune stopped by and noticed dripping wet tablecloths pinned to the clothesline. The girls were taking off their aprons and looking relieved that the task was finally done.

But Mrs. Bethune came right to the point. "Did you boil them?"

Guiltily the girls hung their heads.

Down came the tablecloths from the line. A fire was made, the water boiled, and the cloths went into the pot. "You can never take a shortcut to thoroughness," she told the girls firmly. It was a lesson all the students in Mrs. Bethune's school learned, whether they were conjugating Latin verbs or doing laundry.

Diligence is putting forth your best effort, regardless of the task.

FROM GOD'S WORD:

Whatever work you do, do your best (Ecclesiastes 9:10a).

LET'S TALK ABOUT IT:

1. What do you think Mrs. Bethune meant when she said, "There is no such thing as menial work—only a menial attitude"?
2. What was the result of Mrs. Bethune's educating not only the "head," but also the "hands" and the "hearts" of her students?
3. What kind of work tempts you to take shortcuts? Homework? Chores? Why?

Dignity

"'WHOSOEVER' MEANS YOU!"

Mrs. Mary McLeod Bethune opened her Bible. Sitting in front of her in orderly rows were girls with freshly scrubbed ebony skin, their soft, dark hair brushed and braided, their dark blue skirts and white blouses—the school's uni-form–clean and neat. Some of them were the daughters of clergymen and shopkeepers; others were daughters of railroad workers and day laborers. It didn't matter to Mrs. Bethune. All these girls needed an education. Even more, they needed to know their worth before God after years—centuries—of living in a society that told them they were an inferior race.

"'For God so loved the world,'" Mrs. Bethune read in her rich con-tralto voice, "'that he gave his only begotten Son, that whosoever believeth in him should not perish, but have everlasting life.'" She looked up at the eager faces in front of her. "Did you hear that word, 'whosoever'? That whosoever means you! God loves you so much He sent His Son, Jesus, to die for you. Not just white people. Not just rich people. You! This is where your human dignity comes from—from God, our Creator and Savior."

Mary McLeod Bethune was a good example of dignity. That means she treated everyone, black and white alike, as she would like to be treated. One day she was out knocking on doors in the neighborhood, asking for help for the school. An old white woman came to the door wearing a dirty apron. "Yes, I've heard about your school," she said. "Right nice idea—though I don't 'spect you'll teach 'em much beyond third grade. That's all my pastor says the colored can learn."

Mrs. Bethune winced but did not react to the insult. "I notice you have a cow," she said. "Do you have some milk to spare for the girls?"

"Why, matter of fact, I do," said the old woman. "I churn butter to make ends meet . . . end up having to throw a lot of buttermilk away. You just send up your girls with a pail, and I'll give you all the buttermilk you can use."

Mrs. Bethune smiled broadly. "Thank you very much!"

"Say," said the woman, "I s'pose you can read, being a teacher 'n all. I've . . . uh . . . mislaid my glasses, and I wonder if you could read this letter my son sent me."

Mrs. Bethune—a college graduate—guessed that the woman probably couldn't read herself, but graciously she said nothing and read the woman's letter. It wasn't in her nature to return insult for insult.

Another day, as she was once again knocking on doors telling about the needs of the school, the family happened to be having lunch. Thinking she was a common beggar, the woman said, "Why don't you go into the kitchen, and Ida will give you some lunch."

"Thank you, no," said Mrs. Bethune and moved on to the next house.

The old couple next door was also at lunch, but they invited her to sit down and eat with them. Mrs. Bethune gladly accepted the invitation. While they were enjoying coffee, the woman next door dropped in. Seeing Mrs. Bethune sitting at the table with her hosts, her face reddened. But all Mrs. Bethune did was smile at her graciously.

When young Mary was growing up, white people always called black people by their first names, like children. She never forgot the first time she heard a black person—her first teacher—introduce herself as "Miss Wilson." It gave her a thrill of pride that she resolved to not only extend to others, but to require for herself. After marriage, she always introduced herself as Mrs. Bethune. Many years later, in 1934, she was a delegate to the Southern Conference for Human Welfare. After she proposed an amendment, the chairwoman announced, "Mary's amendment is accepted."

Mrs. Bethune rose and said with simple dignity, "My name is Mrs. Mary McLeod Bethune, and the secretary should record it so."

Dignity means recognizing the basic worth
God gives each one of us, and treating one another with respect.

FROM GOD'S WORD:

So God created human beings in his image. In the image of God he created them (Genesis 1:27a). Show respect for all people (1 Peter 2:17a).

LET'S TALK ABOUT IT:

1. Why was it important for Mrs. Bethune to teach her students that they had dignity as human beings?
2. In what way did Mrs. Bethune show that dignity was a two-way street?
3. Discuss ways you can act with dignity yourself as well as treat others with dignity.

THOMAS A. DORSEY

The Father of Gospel Music

In the first half of the twentieth century, there were two Tommy Dorseys—both renowned musicians. One played trombone and led a big dance band. The other played piano in blues bands. One was white. One was black. One never paid much attention to God, lived the high life, and died at age fifty-one. The other wrestled with God, lived the wild life until he finally surrendered to the Lord, and lived to ninety-three. It was this second Tommy Dorsey—Thomas A. Dorsey—who became the "father of gospel music."

Thomas A. Dorsey was born on July 1, 1899, in rural Georgia. His father was a minister, his mother a music teacher. Money was tight, and when Thomas was about eleven years old, he got a job selling concessions in an Atlanta theater to supplement the family income. There he listened closely to the music and styles of the popular vaudeville acts and learned to play the piano, even teaching himself to read music. On the side, he picked up jobs playing for private parties, calling himself "Barrelhouse Tommy." In spite of his parents' faith, the influence of these settings drew Tommy away from the Lord.

At age seventeen, he hit the road determined to make it on his own.

He landed in Chicago, playing local gin joints. But he also married Nettie Harper and enrolled in the Chicago School of Composition and Arranging to improve his skills. In time, he was hired by a record company to arrange songs and scout new talent. He also began writing songs that various blues singers began recording. He put together his Wildcats Jazz Band to back the popular blues singer Ma Rainey, and off they went on tour. His professional name was now "Georgia Tom," and the lyrics of his songs were often sexually suggestive. "Tight Like That" (1928) sold over seven million copies.

Success seemed to have arrived, but one night onstage, Dorsey noticed an "unsteadiness" in his playing. It grew worse until he couldn't perform or write music. He fell into a deep depression. Neither doctors nor rest helped. He considered suicide. Then he began thinking more seriously about God and the faith of his youth. At the urging of his sister-in-law, he went to church, where he was miraculously healed.

Dorsey committed himself to the Lord and wrote his first "gospel" song. Though it later became a favorite, he was not immediately accepted. His blending of old blues and jazz riffs with the gospel message appealed to listeners, but church leaders accused him of bringing the "world" into the church. "I've been thrown out of some of the best churches in the country," he later joked.

Then in 1932 he accepted the position of choir director at Chicago's large Pilgrim Baptist Church, where he continued to serve for forty years. This gave him a platform for sharing his new "gospel music" and for traveling and ministering elsewhere.

The next year he also founded the National Convention of Gospel Choirs and Choruses to help musicians develop their skills. Over the years Dorsey wrote hundreds of gospel songs performed by musicians as diverse as Mahalia Jackson, Aretha Franklin, and Elvis Presley. His songs include such classics as "Take My Hand, Precious Lord," "Peace in the Valley," and "It's a Highway to Heaven." But perhaps his greatest contribution was that he set the stage for today's contemporary Christian musicians to use whatever style works best to spread the Gospel.

"But I can't take credit for this stuff," Dorsey said. "I'm only human, and these things are the makings of God. Everything I do—everything that's good, at least—is a reflection of his hand."

Surrender

TAMING A WILD CAT

When a situation seems completely unmanageable, we sometimes say, "It's like herding cats," because cats don't easily yield to our direction. They pretty much do what they want and cooperate only to get what they want . . . like coming to get fed.

Thomas A. Dorsey was a wild cat. He even called his jazz band the Wild Cats and thought up cool-cat names for himself: "Barrelhouse Tom," "Texas Tommy," and "Georgia Tom." And he hung with cats like Tampa Red, Scrapper Blackwell, Big Bill Broonzy, Frankie Jaxson, and Blind Lemon Jefferson.

Tommy had been born into a Christian home where he heard the Gospel and knew right from wrong. And God planned to tame and reclaim him.

It began one evening in 1926 in a club on Chicago's far south side where Tommy was playing with his band. Suddenly, he felt unsure of himself as he played. At first it didn't stop him completely, but it sapped his confidence. The uneasiness grew until he was sure the other cats in the band would notice his hesitance and think he was drunk or on drugs. But that wasn't it. His thoughts were just falling in on themselves.

He went home hoping he would feel better the next morning, or maybe he was just coming down with the flu. But he felt worse the next day. Confusion overwhelmed him and left him unable to know where to turn for help.

"I wanted comfort for my wife," he later said, "yet I could only take it from her. Our money was soon gone. We had no income and no one to look to for help. I went from doctor to doctor; they could not find anything wrong with me. I became a pitiful sight, weighing only one hundred seventeen pounds and looking like a skeleton."

The band got another piano player, and Tommy's career seemed over. Nettie took a job in a laundry and came home at night to nurse him. "I did not seem to improve. I was perplexed, sick, disturbed, and a bundle of confusion."

One day he walked down to Lake Michigan and stood there, thinking about jumping in and ending it all. What else was there to do? But somehow he made it home.

That Saturday evening, Nettie's sister said, "Why don't you come to church with me tomorrow, Tommy. You know the Lord hasn't forgotten you, and He's a healer."

That night he thought more about God than he had in many years. And the next morning, he said later, the minister zeroed right in on him as soon as he got to church. "Bishop H. H. Haley walked right up to me and spoke gently and quietly: 'Brother Dorsey, there is no reason for you to be looking so poorly and feeling so badly. The Lord has too much work for you to do to let you die. Can I pray for you?'

"What could I do? I yielded."

Instantly, Thomas was healed, and he went home a new man, growing stronger physically, mentally, and spiritually. But what kind of work did the Lord have in mind?

Surrender requires yielding to God's superior power and accepting his correction.

FROM GOD'S WORD:

We have all had human fathers who disciplined us and we respected them for it. How much more should we submit to the Father of our spirits and live! (Hebrews 12:9 NIV).

LET'S TALK ABOUT IT:

1. How do you think being brought up in a Christian home influenced Thomas Dorsey?
2. In Jesus' parable about the Prodigal Son (Luke 15:11–24), the youngest son had to go through some pretty hard times before he "came to his senses." How was this similar to Thomas Dorsey's experience?
3. Tell about a time when you were "forced" to change your ways and do what was right. Later, were you glad you changed? Why?

Submission

"TAKE MY HAND, PRECIOUS LORD"

Shortly after Thomas Dorsey was healed from the depression that had so handicapped him, the man living in the apartment below the Dorseys got sick one morning and died by evening. It was a great shock to Thomas. He recalled thinking, "I couldn't understand! I had been sick nearly two years and this young man was sick for just one day, and then he died. My mind went back to what the minister told me when my sister-in-law took me to church. His words—though they had been spoken quietly—thundered in my ears: 'Have more faith! You will not die! The Lord has a great work for you to do.'"

His friend's sudden death caused Thomas to want to know what "great work" God had in mind for him. Music was all he knew, and a certain kind of music at that, the kind that moved people's souls and spoke to their hearts. Dorsey began thinking about the possibility of writing sacred music based on those riffs and rhythms that featured syncopated notes in an eight-bar blues structure. But instead of themes of despair and defiance, he would tell stories of hope and affirmation. "It'll be *good news*," he said. "So I'll call it 'gospel music.' Doesn't 'gospel' mean good news?"

His first gospel song was one about the assurance of salvation. "If You See My Savior, Tell Him That You Saw Me" actually told the story of standing at the bedside of his neighbor and asking him to do him the favor when he got to heaven of telling Jesus that "when you saw me, I was on my way," and that "I'm coming home someday."

But many church leaders accused him of bringing the "world" into the church with his bouncy blues tune. At the time, the rejection so discouraged him that he went back to writing some more secular songs just to make a living. Then in 1932 he accepted the position of choir director at Chicago's large Pilgrim Baptist Church, where he continued to serve for forty years. Having a recognized ministry position there led to invitations to minister elsewhere. In August he was invited to go to St. Louis and be the featured soloist at a large revival meeting. His wife, Nettie, was due to give birth soon, and something in his spirit told him not to go. But it seemed like such a great opportunity to introduce gospel music that he went anyway.

The crowd received his music enthusiastically and asked for more and more. But when he finally sat down, a messenger handed him a telegram: "YOUR WIFE JUST DIED."

He raced home in unbelieving shock, only to find that it was true. Then, two days later, his newly born baby boy died as well. The double tragedy threw Dorsey back into the bottomless pit of depression. "I felt God had done me an injustice," he said. "I didn't want to serve him anymore or write gospel songs. I just wanted to go back to that jazz world I once knew so well."

But a friend knew what Thomas needed and arranged for him to be left alone in a room with a piano. He recalled, "As I hunched alone there in the dark, I thought back to the afternoon I went to St. Louis. Something kept telling me to stay with Nettie. Was that something God? Oh, if I had paid more attention to him that day, I would have stayed and been with Nettie…. From that moment on I vowed to listen more closely to him."

There in the quietness, Dorsey reached out to the Lord and composed his greatest hit, "Take My Hand, Precious Lord," which has ministered to tens of thousands of other people in their grief.

Submission is more than surrendering to a superior power. It requires putting your hand in the Lord's and letting Him lead.

FROM GOD'S WORD:

[Jesus] prayed, "Father, if you are willing, take this cup from me; yet not my will, but yours be done" (Luke 22:42 NIV).

LET'S TALK ABOUT IT:

1. There's a story about a rambunctious little boy who was made to sit down in school, but he said, "Inside, I'm still standing up." Had he submitted or surrendered? Explain.
2. What was the "great work" God had in mind for Thomas Dorsey?
3. In a hymnal or online, find the words to "Take My Hand, Precious Lord" (sometimes called "Precious Lord, Take My Hand"), and explain how that song could comfort someone who is very sad.

Excellence

"WHEN I'VE DONE MY BEST"

When his first efforts to introduce his new "gospel songs" in church settings were rejected by most ministers, Thomas A. Dorsey opened the first black gospel music publishing company, Dorsey House of Music, and resorted to the distribution methods he had known when selling his old blues tunes. He explained, "I borrowed five dollars and sent out five hundred copies of my song 'If You See My Savior' to churches throughout the country. But it was three years before I got a single order."

So he took a more personal approach and sent his first business partner, gospel singer Sallie Martin, to churches from coast to coast. She either tried to sell his song sheets directly to their choir directors or offered to be a guest soloist for Sunday morning . . . of course singing Dorsey's songs.

But as skilled as Dorsey was in promoting his music as well as gospel music that began being written by other people, he was less careful about collecting royalties. In fact, it was probably the feisty Sallie Martin who kept Dorsey's business solvent. Nevertheless, he was so forward looking that he didn't notice that some of his songs began to show up under the names of other composers, black and white. A recent example of this is his 1928 song "If You See My Savior," which appears with only a couple minor variations under the title "Standin' by the Bedside" on the Dixie Chicks' *Little Ol' Cowgirl* album and is attributed to the 1992 work of Ira Tucker of the Dixie Hummingbirds.

In 1937 Mahalia Jackson took over Martin's place and continued to tour with Dorsey until 1944. Dorsey wrote his song "Peace in the Valley" specifically for Jackson, and the period became known as "The Golden Age of Gospel." When his songs "Take My Hand, Precious Lord" and "Peace in the Valley" began being recorded by white singers such as Red Foley and Elvis Presley, they became as popular in white congregations as black.

The National Convention of Gospel Choirs and Choruses was one of Dorsey's attempts to encourage other musicians. And yet as one of his songs suggests, he seemed never satisfied that he had done enough.

When I've done the best I can,
If my friends don't understand,
Then my Lord will carry me home.

But the NCGCC, which is still going strong today, recognizes its founder not only as the "father of gospel music" but as the man who "cultivated a standard of excellence in the gospel music industry. His music was deeply rooted in scriptures and was connected to everyday life experiences. He had a passion and commitment to support the local church by training songwriters, musicians, directors, and singers to enhance the church's ministry through music."

In God's eyes, excellence is doing the best you can.

FROM GOD'S WORD:

I have fought the good fight, I have finished the race, I have kept the faith. Now there is in store for me the crown of righteousness, which the Lord, the righteous Judge, will award to me on that day (2 Timothy 4:7–8 NIV).

LET'S TALK ABOUT IT:

1. What did Thomas Dorsey do when his music wasn't first accepted?
2. How is helping others one of the best things we can do?
3. Why do people sometimes misunderstand whether you are doing your best?

ELIZA DAVIS GEORGE

Liberia's American "Mother"

Eliza Davis was born in Texas on January 20, 1879, and died in Texas in 1979—one hundred years later. Living to be a hundred years old is a remarkable thing, but not nearly as remarkable as how Eliza spent those years.

For most African Americans after the Civil War, life was a constant struggle. Poverty, lack of education, and continuing discrimination were the critical issues facing black leaders well into the twentieth century. But to Eliza Davis, American blacks had one source of wealth worth sharing: the Gospel of Jesus Christ. While studying for her teaching certificate, Eliza heard a pastor who had just returned from Liberia. "The people are lost in pagan religions because no one has taken the Gospel to them. Who will go? White missionaries, you say? These are *our* people! *Our* ancestors! *We* have a responsibility to share the Good News with our brothers and sisters in Africa."

The pastor's words burned deep in Eliza's heart. She finished college and taught school for several years, but "the call" grew stronger. She had to go to Africa.

Eliza Davis turned thirty-five the day the ship *Celtic* nosed into the docks of Monrovia on January 20, 1914. The coast of Liberia had several "civilized" cities of "Americo-Liberians"—former American slaves, or descendents of slaves, who had returned to their homeland—and many churches. But Eliza turned her heart to the native tribal people in the interior who had never heard of Jesus.

Her vision was to teach the children, whom she hoped would teach their own people. But in 1917, the National Baptist Association sent a married couple to replace her at the school she had established. What was she going to do now?

Eliza got a startling proposal from a black gentleman, a British citizen: "I'll help you start a new mission if you'll marry me." Eliza married G. Thompson George on January 12, 1918, and together they established the Kelton Mission. She became "Mother George" to hundreds of children, several of whom she adopted as her own and even brought to the United States for further education.

But money from Eliza's supporters arrived only sporadically. Several times Eliza and "Mr. George" traveled back to the United States to speak to churches and raise support. Often Mother George returned to Liberia, only to find the mission buildings destroyed by termites and the people scattered. She had to begin the work all over again.

Still, Eliza held on to her vision of training Liberians to teach Liberians. And finally all the seeds she had sown in the stubborn soil of Liberia took root. The Elizabeth Native Interior Mission (ENI) became the umbrella for many schools for tribal children, as well as a maternity clinic; the Eliza Davis George Pastor's Training School sent out hundreds of native church leaders to establish churches.

For her labor of love, Mother George was awarded a knighthood and a citation as "Grande Dame Commander" in the Republic of Liberia shortly before her death on March 8, 1979. "One hundred years old is old enough."

Perseverance

TWO HUNDRED MILES BY
ANKLE-EXPRESS

Mother Eliza George finished the pile of mending and glanced at the noonday sun beating down on the wood and thatch buildings in the jungle clearing. It was time to call the children together for prayer.

Lifting her strong, clear voice, Mother George began to sing, "Jesus, Keep Me Near the Cross." All over Kelton Mission, children of all ages stopped what they were doing and ran toward the thin, brown-skinned American woman whom they called "Mother." As they clustered around her, she began to pray for each of the children by name. Then came prayers that Mr. George would come back to Liberia soon and that their supporters in America would send the money they so desperately needed to pay their debts and buy food, clothes, and schoolbooks for the children.

As the children settled down to their meager noon meal of rice and vegetables, a man appeared out of the jungle. "Mother," he called, "a steamer arrived yesterday in Greenville. Maybe . . ."

The words were hardly out of his mouth before Mother George jumped up, disappeared inside her thatched-roof house, and reappeared wearing her sun helmet and big rubber boots for walking the jungle trails. "Maude," she told her eighteen-year-old adopted daughter, "see that the children keep on with their lessons and chores. Robert and Tussnah, you come with me. We're going for the mail!"

Walking the twenty miles to Greenville was not unusual for Mother George. She often tramped from village to village by "ankle-express," as she laughingly called it, sharing the Gospel. Today she hardly noticed the miles as they slogged their way through the swampy jungle. Surely there would be money waiting for them.

When the trio finally arrived, Mother George marched directly to the post office. "Any mail for Mother?" The clerk handed her a batch of letters . . . yes! A letter from Mr. George. She ripped open the envelope but found only a letter. *"One of the churches sent you $200. I hope you have received it."*

Had she missed something? But all she found was a notice from the post office in Monrovia: *"A postal order for $200 has been received for you. Please pick it up within thirty days."* Monrovia? The capital city was two hundred miles away! Frantically, Mother George looked at the date the notice had been sent. Four weeks ago! Was it too late?

"Robert . . . Tussnah, come. We have no time to lose. We're going to Monrovia."

The boys looked confused. "But, Mother, the steamer has already left. We have no way to get there."

"Oh yes, we do." Her eyes had a determined look. "Ankle-express." And so the trio set off along the beach, heading north. Each long, hot day blurred into the next. The cool seawater soothed their burning, blistered feet. Fishermen and villagers along the way gave them a meal or a grass mat for the night. They often had to wait for the tide to go out before they could get around a rocky point.

Finally, six days later, their feet swollen and bleeding, Mother George and the two boys dragged into Monrovia and made their way to the post office. Wearily, Mother handed the clerk the notice about the postal order.

The clerk frowned. "I'm sorry, Mrs. George. No one came to claim it, so we sent it back to the United States last week."

Tussnah broke down with a loud wail. Mother George wiped away her own tears of disappointment. Should she give up now? No! Hadn't God brought her to Liberia? Her work wasn't finished yet. Somehow, sometime, some way, God would provide the money to keep the mission school going. But right now, all she could do was return home again the same way she had come—by ankle-express.

Perseverance often depends on how strongly we believe in our goal.

FROM GOD'S WORD:

Love never gives up, never loses faith, is always hopeful, and endures through every circumstance (1 Corinthians 13:7 NLT).

LET'S TALK ABOUT IT:

1. What did you think was going to happen when Mother George finally got to Monrovia?
2. How do you usually react when something you want very much doesn't happen? (Give up? Get mad? Blame God?)
3. Discuss: Sometimes we say God is "shutting a door" when things don't happen the way we had hoped. Other times, God wants us to keep hold of our goal, even when bad things happen. How do we know the difference?

Encouragement

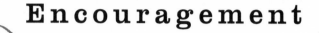

SNIP AND STITCH

Bam! Bam! The teenage boy pounded the last post into the ground with his big wooden mallet and stood back to look at the sturdy fence. *That* should keep the forest "critters" out of the mission garden.

"Good job, Charles Carpenter," came a woman's voice. Charles jumped. He hadn't heard Mother George come up behind him. The American missionary was grinning from ear to ear. "You are certainly living up to your name! You are a hard worker."

Embarrassed, Charles looked at his bare toes. He had lived in the forests of Liberia his whole life up till now and still wasn't used to his new name and the "civilized ways" here at Kelton Mission. But he liked this American woman whose skin was the same color as his own and who treated him no differently than the town boys who came to her school. But . . . there was something that bothered him.

"What is it, son?" she said, as if reading his mind.

He felt his ears burn. "I . . . my clothes . . ." He was ashamed of the tattered pants he'd been wearing ever since he arrived at the mission.

"Of course! You need a new pair of pants. Mercy me, why didn't I think of this before?"

The next day Charles scurried along the jungle trail toward Greenville with money in his pocket for a new pair of pants. He felt like a grown man walking into the tailor's shop to order his own pair of pants.

The tailor was busy with another customer. Charles waited and waited. The other customer left. Still Charles waited. Finally he cleared his throat. "I would like to order—"

"What? Get out! Shoo, shoo," said the tailor. "Don't want no country boys in my shop."

"But I have money—"

"Money? You probably stole it. Go on, now, get out." And the door slammed firmly behind him.

Humiliated, Charles walked the twenty miles back to Kelton Mission.

When he told Mother George what had happened, her eyes got a determined look. "Then you shall learn to sew yourself!" she announced.

The next day, Charles found himself on the trail back to Greenville with money in his pocket for room and food. He found a different tailor and asked if he could watch. For several weeks, he hung around the shop, watching the tailor measure and snip and sew. Then he went back to the mission and reported what he'd been learning.

Mother George gave him a piece of cloth and a pair of scissors and sent him back to Greenville. Now when the tailor measured, he measured; when he cut, Charles cut. Back at the mission he stitched up the pants. What a mess! The seams were bunched and crooked. But Mother George held them up and said, "You are learning so fast! I know that you will soon be sewing clothes for the whole mission!"

Back to Greenville. This time Charles watched and measured and cut even more carefully. This time the pants he sewed up were much better. Again and again he practiced. And the next time a bolt of cloth arrived at the mission, Mother George handed the whole bolt to Charles and said casually, "The little boys need new pants."

Many years later, Charles married Lu, a mission girl whom Mother George had taken under her wing, and she sent out the young couple to establish another school for children in the forest. Looking back, Charles said, "I was an ignorant country boy, but Mother George believed in me. From that time on, I made a special effort to please her, because she believed I was just as important to God as the town boys."

An encourager sees people as God sees them—
each person has value, with gifts and talents that need to be encouraged.

FROM GOD'S WORD:

So encourage each other and build each other up, just as you are already doing (1 Thessalonians 5:11 NLT).

LET'S TALK ABOUT IT:

1. What qualities in Charles did Mother George see that made her confident that he could learn to be a tailor?
2. In what ways did she encourage him? (Make a list!)
3. Is there someone you could encourage today? How?

Sacrifice

"SON, TAKE IT"

Mother Eliza Davis George proudly listened to Augustus Marwieh deliver the valedictory speech for the 1953 graduating class of the College of Liberia. Could this really be the same "country boy" who had come to her mission when he was only fifteen? Even though he was the son of a tribal chief, he couldn't read or write. Now look at him!

Ever since Mother George had come to Africa, she'd had a dream—that a young Liberian from the "uncivilized" tribes would be educated, trained, and then come back to be a missionary to his own people. Mother knew she was getting old. She needed someone who could take over her work.

She had taken several promising girls to America to be educated. But one got sick and died, one married an American, one liked "town life." But Gus . . . surely Gus was the one God had chosen to take over her work. As the old woman and young man walked the jungle trails to visit the villagers, she listened as he shared the great burden he had for his own people. Yes, yes, Gus was the one.

Mother George eagerly followed Gus's progress as he continued his schooling in America—first Simpson College, then Golden Gate Seminary in San Francisco. When Mother had to return to the U.S. for an emergency eye operation, she thought, *I'll surprise Gus and go see him!*

But she wasn't prepared for the surprise he had for her. "Mother, this is Donna," Gus said, introducing a lovely American girl. "We are in love, and she has agreed to marry me and come to Africa with me to work in the mission."

Sadly, Mother George shook her head. "Oh, dear young people. This is not God's choice for you. Donna may think she shares your call to return to your people in the jungles of Liberia. But mission life is hard. One day you will be forced to choose between God's call and a wife who will be homesick and not used to the rigors of jungle life."

Gus felt heartbroken. But he respected Mother too much to ignore her advice. Sadly, he and Donna broke their engagement. Then, on Mother's advice, he chose a fine young woman from the ENI mission to be his bride—a girl named Othelia.

Mother George was still on furlough when Gus sailed back to Africa in 1960 to meet his bride and take up duties at the mission. But a letter from Gus soon found her in Texas. *"Dr. William Tolbert has asked me to be assistant principal of the Liberian Baptist school in Monrovia. They are desperate for qualified staff. What should I do, Mother?"*

As Mother George read the letter, she felt her hopes crumbling. Dr. William Tolbert was the vice-president of Liberia, as well as president of the Liberian Baptist Association. Why did she think she could keep such a brilliant and well-educated young man as Augustus Marwieh for her own little mission out in the bush? But she was eighty-one years old. Who would take over the mission now?

Eliza Davis George fell to her knees in prayer and committed the ENI mission to God. Then she got off her knees and sent a telegram to Gus: *"Son, take it."*

Gus took the job. But he couldn't stop thinking about his people in the forests of Liberia. Five years later he resigned. What a joyous homecoming at the mission! Now Mother George could rest, knowing that her work would be in Gus's capable hands.

"What did Othelia say?" asked Mother George. She knew it wasn't easy to give up their nice house and car and good salary in Monrovia to return to the forest, where many villages still could only be reached by "ankle-express."

Gus grinned. "You picked a good wife for me, Mother. Othelia said, 'If God is leading us to go, let's go.'"

Sometimes we have to sacrifice our own plans and trust God to work things out in His own way and His own time.

FROM GOD'S WORD:

"Father . . . not my will, but yours be done" (Luke 22:42 NIV).

LET'S TALK ABOUT IT:

1. Why did Mother George think Gus Marwieh was the person God intended to take over the mission work when she got too old?
2. Why do you think Mother George advised Gus to take the job, even though she had to sacrifice her own hopes for him? How did God work it out?
3. Parents, share with your children a time when you had to "let go" of your own plans and trust God to work things out. What was the result?

DR. MARTIN LUTHER KING JR.

Civil Rights Leader

Dr. Martin Luther King Jr. was first of all a preacher, the son of a preacher, and even the grandson of a preacher—all of them having served the Dexter Avenue Baptist Church in Montgomery, Alabama. In addition to the guidance and example of his father and maternal grandfather, Martin trained at Morehouse College in Atlanta and Crozer Theological Seminary in Chester, Pennsylvania, and he received his PhD in systematic theology from Boston University in 1955.

Prior to this time, African Americans were denied equal rights in much of the South. In fact, there were laws known as "Jim Crow Laws" that prohibited them from mixing with white people. They couldn't eat in the same restaurants, drink from the same public fountains, use the same rest rooms, or ride in the same part of a bus. Blacks were to sit in the back of the bus or even stand, while the more convenient seats near the front were reserved for whites.

Knowing such laws were unfair, many African-American leaders were waiting for an opportunity to test their legality, confident that if the test case got to the United States Supreme Court, the bad laws would be over-turned. The opportunity came on December 1, 1955, when Rosa Parks, a seamstress in Montgomery, Alabama, refused to move to the back of the bus when ordered to do so.

Black residents formed the Montgomery Improvement Association, elected Dr. King—with his newly earned PhD—as its president, and five days later they launched a bus boycott in which the black people of Mont-gomery refused to ride the buses until the unfair laws were changed. Since three-fourths of the bus passengers were African American, the boycott meant a major financial loss for the bus companies.

Knowing Dr. King was a leader of the boycott, angry white separatists fire-bombed his home, the home of his associate Ralph Abernathy, and four black Baptist churches. Dr. King was arrested and convicted along with other boycott leaders on charges of conspiring to interfere with the bus company's operations. Despite these attempts to suppress the move-ment, Montgomery buses were desegregated in December 1956, after the United States Supreme Court declared Alabama's segregation laws regarding public transportation unconstitutional.

Because God is the source of all righteousness, Dr. King believed his concern for civil rights grew directly from his faith. His grandfather, Rev. A. D. Williams, and father, Martin Luther King Sr., were both civil rights leaders, with Williams having founded Atlanta's chapter of the NAACP. Nevertheless, Dr. King's outstanding skills as a preacher and his God-given courage elevated him to national leadership. His nonviolent approach was similar to what happened in the early church where the Greek-speaking believers complained against those who spoke Hebrew, saying that their widows were being discriminated against in the daily distribution of food. When it was brought to the attention of the apostles, they acknowledged the injustice and corrected it. Dr. King believed if he could show how unjustly blacks were being treated, the country—and particularly the Supreme Court—would respond with justice.

Therefore he led many demonstrations calling attention to injustices. Often evil and misguided people responded with violence, and local governments frequently arrested Dr. King and his followers. But slowly the laws—and later even attitudes—began to change.

On August 28, 1963, 250,000 people gathered before the Lincoln Memorial in Washington, D.C., where Dr. King delivered his famous "I Have a Dream" speech. It concluded with the hopeful words of the old Negro spiritual, "Free at last! Free at last! Thank God Almighty, we are free at last!"

For over a dozen years, Dr. King led the struggle for equal rights for all people until he was martyred on April 4, 1968, at the relatively young age of thirty-nine.

Dignity

THE BIRTH OF A DREAM

Martin Luther King Jr. was born on January 15, 1929, into a comfortable home in Atlanta, Georgia, with two bathrooms and plenty of space for the whole family, including his older sister, Willie Christine, and his younger brother, Albert Daniel. But the family was not so far removed from poverty that Martin did not hear stories from his father about the hard life as a sharecropper.

Martin's father was the second of ten children who had grown up working hard and earning barely enough to pay last year's bill. At age sixteen, Martin's father left the farm in Stockbridge, Georgia, to find a better life in the big city of Atlanta. He arrived with only a sixth-grade education, but he worked hard and continued to study on the side until church people noticed how well he could preach. In time he married the daughter of Rev. Adam Daniel Williams, the pastor of the Ebenezer Baptist Church. When Martin Jr. was born, his father was a full-time minister with a middle-class salary.

But having money isn't always enough to bring dignity. One day while Martin was riding beside his dad in the car, his father accidentally ran a stop sign. An observant police officer pulled him over, but when he saw that the driver was black, he sneered. "All right, *boy,* let me see your license."

Calling a grown man a boy was a common insult, intended to remind African Americans that they weren't accepted as equals.

Rev. King clinched his lips. His eyes flashed as he pointed to Martin. "This is a boy. I'm a man. Until you address me as such, I will not listen to you."

The shocked policeman mumbled something about uppity blacks, quickly wrote out the ticket, and left.

His father turned to Martin. "I don't care how long I have to live with this system," he said, "but I will never accept it." Young Martin knew his father had been lucky. Segregation bred violence, and he had seen the Ku Klux Klan burn crosses on people's lawns at night and beat or kill them if they didn't submit to the system. His father could have received far worse than a ticket that day.

Martin had already experienced the bite of segregation when white parents wouldn't let their children play with him and when he had to go to a separate school. Later, he attended an oratory contest in Valdosta, Georgia, where he took second prize. But on the long ride home to Atlanta, he and all the other black people had to stand up so there could be enough seats for the white people on the bus.

These experiences almost caused Martin to hate all white people. Instead, within him was born a dream of growing up to a life of God-given dignity, and he would never waver in his quest to achieve that dream when—as he would later say—"all of God's children, black men and white men, Jews and Gentiles, Protestants and Catholics, will be able to join hands" and live in freedom and dignity.

He knew his path would require a good education, and he studied so hard in high school he was able to skip two grades and enter Morehouse Collage at the age of fifteen. Two of his college professors were ministers who encouraged him that the Gospel held the greatest hope for defeating segregation and poverty. After all, the Scriptures declared all believers were of equal value in the Body of Christ regardless of race or status.

At eighteen, Martin became an assistant minister under his father at Ebenezer Baptist Church in Atlanta while he continued his studies, graduating from Morehouse and later from seminary in Pennsylvania where he was one of only six blacks. He earned straight A's, proving what his mother had once said: "You are as good as anybody."

Martin met and married Coretta Scott and began working on his PhD. In 1954 he was called to be the pastor of the Dexter Avenue Baptist Church in Montgomery, Alabama. God was positioning him for his greatest ministry.

Dignity is given when people follow the Golden Rule: "Do to others what you would have them do to you" (Matthew 7:12 NIV).

FROM GOD'S WORD:

Some of us are Jews, some are Gentiles, some are slaves, and some are free. But we have all been baptized into Christ's body by one Spirit, and we have all received the same Spirit (1 Corinthians 12:13 NLT).

LET'S TALK ABOUT IT:

1. Why was calling a man a "boy" disrespectful?
2. Instead of hating all white people for how they treated black people, what was Martin Luther King Jr.'s dream? How did he set about preparing himself to fulfill that dream?
3. How does the Bible teach us to treat other people, regardless of race or status?

Nonviolence

THE POWER OF
TURNING THE OTHER CHEEK

For Dr. King, the victory of the Montgomery bus boycott was only one step on the road to freedom. There were many other areas in the South where segregation was enforced by local laws and customs. Dr. King and the other leaders knew that in keeping the races apart, the segregationists preserved the myth of black inferiority and white superiority. If the races were allowed to mix freely, in time people would realize there are smart and dumb people, brave and cowardly people, good and evil people within all races. Once that truth was accepted, the fear of other races would subside and hopefully the violence designed to keep "them" in their place would diminish.

So there were far more important goals for the Civil Rights Movement than merely the freedom to buy a hamburger at an "all white" lunch counter!

But they had to start somewhere.

Dr. King knew that the Bible told us to "Defend the cause of the weak and fatherless; maintain the rights of the poor and oppressed (Psalm 82:3 NIV). But how was he to do that when the rights of the poor and oppressed were denied by law and custom? In school, he had studied the writings of Henry David Thoreau and the experiences of Mahatma Gandhi. Both men believed in the legitimacy of nonviolent disobedience as a means of challenging and overturning unjust laws. Gandhi had used these peaceful tactics to gain India's independence from Britain. Indians had marched, gone on strike, boycotted British goods, and even sat down in the streets to bring business to a stop . . . all for the purpose of drawing the world's attention to injustice. He knew if the British responded with force against the unarmed people, the world would disapprove and force Britain to yield. It worked, and in 1947 Britain gave India its independence.

Dr. King recalled how Jesus had responded when attacked and taken by force. He could have called ten thousand angels to his defense, yet he submitted without physical resistance. Hadn't Gandhi been following Jesus' example of nonviolence? Dr. King also realized that in this modern age of television and news media, any violent response by local officials toward peaceful demonstrators would only make the officials look bad, and that would bring pressure from the rest of the country for them to change.

The leaders of the Movement selected Birmingham, Alabama, as one of the cruelest cities toward black people and decided to focus there. Dr. King led Birmingham's African Americans in marches, sit-ins, and pray-ins. They refused to buy at downtown stores with segregated lunch counters and washrooms. Day by day the protests grew larger until the jails were filled with hundreds and then thousands of peaceful protesters, many of them school children. Dr. King himself voluntarily submitted to being arrested and thrown in jail. Finally, the city officials began responding with force. They used dogs and fire hoses with water pressure powerful enough to rip the bark off of trees, break bones, and roll human bodies across streets. White people, seeing the shocking events on TV, joined the protests. Unfortunately, some of the African-American bystanders, untrained in nonviolence, were unable to restrain their anger and began throwing rocks and bottles at the police. In an attempt to inflame further violence, segregationists bombed the hotel where Dr. King had been staying and the home of his brother. Neither were hurt, but a full-scale riot threatened.

Finally, on May 10, 1963, with pressure from President John F. Kennedy, white businessmen finally made some concessions to black demands. Dr. King wanted to avoid further violence and agreed to accept the compromises, declaring victory in Birmingham.

The Birmingham crusade affected black people everywhere. Spontaneous protests erupted in hundreds of cities. Black people were tired of suffering and waiting. They wanted an end to segregation, the right to vote, and good jobs. But four months later, the Ku Klux Klan exploded a bomb in the Sixteenth Street Baptist Church of Birmingham, which had been the hub of the Birmingham crusade. It killed four young girls.

*"The reason I can't follow the old eye-for-an-eye philosophy
is that it ends up leaving everybody blind."*
—Dr. Martin Luther King Jr.,
on the steps of the Sixteenth Street Baptist Church, May 3, 1963

FROM GOD'S WORD:

"But I [Jesus] tell you, Do not resist an evil person. If someone strikes you on the right cheek, turn to him the other also" (Matthew 5:39 NIV).

LET'S TALK ABOUT IT:

1. Why did the Civil Rights Movement want to end segregation?
2. What role did television and the media play in the success of the Birmingham crusade?
3. Why do you think Jesus told us to turn the other cheek if someone strikes us?

Self-Sacrifice

"I'M SO HAPPY THAT YOU DIDN'T SNEEZE!"

In 1958 a woman walked up to Dr. King while he was signing autographs of his book about the Montgomery bus boycott and stabbed him in the chest. The blade went in so far that the tip was on the edge of his aorta, the main artery leaving his heart. After surgery to repair the wound, the doctors told Dr. King that if he had merely sneezed before they removed it surgically, he would have bled to death in moments. But he hadn't sneezed, and God restored him to full health so he could complete his mission.

The person who stabbed him was not a Ku Klux Klan member. In fact, she was just a mentally disturbed person and a black woman at that. Nevertheless, his injury received national media attention, and many people sent him cards and get-well wishes. One was from a ninth-grade girl: "While it should not matter, I would like to mention that I am a white girl.... And I'm simply writing you to say that I'm so happy that you didn't sneeze." He never forgot those encouraging words.

During his life, King received continual death threats, was attacked with stones and frequently arrested, had his house bombed, and was investigated by the FBI (under the presumption he was a communist). Still, throughout the struggle for racial justice, he prayed that God would remove all bitterness from his heart and would give him the strength and courage to face any disaster that came his way. And God granted him that peace.

Ten years after the stabbing, while giving a speech in Memphis, Tennessee, Dr. King said, "I am happy that I didn't sneeze. Because if I had sneezed, I wouldn't have been around" to take part in moving America closer to the dream he had spoken of on the steps of the Lincoln Memorial when a quarter of a million Americans marched on Washington in support of civil rights reforms. In those ten years, numerous civil rights workers had been murdered, and countless protesters had been beaten and jailed. Nevertheless, segregation laws had been declared unconstitutional. The Civil Rights Bill of 1964 was passed, as was the Voting Rights Act of 1965. And though the country was still divided, attitudes were changing in support of racial justice and concern for the poor.

But in that same Memphis speech, Dr. King also spoke as though God had given him a prophetic vision into what was to come his way "from some sick white brothers," as he called them. Nevertheless, he added, "It really doesn't matter what happens now." He knew he had completed his part, the assignment God had given him.

He went on to say, "Well, I don't know what will happen now. We've got some difficult days ahead. But it doesn't matter with me now. Because I've been to the mountaintop. And I don't mind. Like anybody, I would like to live a long life. Longevity has its place. But I'm not concerned about that now. I just want to do God's will. And He's allowed me to go up to the mountain. And I've looked over. And I've seen the promised land. I may not get there with you. But I want you to know tonight, that we, as a people, will get to the promised land. And I'm happy, tonight. I'm not worried about anything. I'm not fearing any man. Mine eyes have seen the glory of the coming of the Lord."

The next afternoon, Dr. King stepped out on the balcony of the Lorraine Motel, where he and his colleagues were staying while they were in Memphis. He called to Ben Branch, a musician who was scheduled to play for a rally that evening. "Ben, make sure you play 'Take My Hand, Precious Lord,' in the meeting tonight. Play it real pretty."

Moments later shots rang out from a rifleman across the road.

It was Mahalia Jackson who sang King's favorite, "Take My Hand, Precious Lord," five days later at his funeral.

Confidence that God is in control is the only rationale for self-sacrifice.

FROM GOD'S WORD:

Greater love has no one than this, that he lay down his life for his friends (John 15:13 NIV).

LET'S TALK ABOUT IT:

1. Why do you think God kept Dr. King from sneezing after he was stabbed?
2. Do you think Dr. King knew he was going to die? Why?
3. How can someone sacrifice themselves for others even if they don't have to die for them?

JOHN PERKINS

A Man Hate Couldn't Stop

The Perkins family were sharecroppers like most blacks in Mississippi in the 1930s and 1940s. Some were also bootleggers and gamblers—and unlike most black folks who were afraid to cross "The Man" (white people), "a Perkins ain't afraid to stand up to nobody."

John Perkins was tough, too. He had to be. His mama died in 1930 when he was only seven months old, and his daddy took off, leaving the kids in the care of John's grandmother. John wasn't religious, but he hung around the country church because that was the only place black folks could get together and socialize.

But when his older brother, Clyde, was shot and killed by a white deputy while standing outside a movie theater, the family sent sixteen-year-old John to California for his own safety. It was a chance to start over, away from the open racism of the South, and he knew how to work hard. Soon the school dropout was experiencing a new feeling—success. Eventually, John married his sweetheart from back home, brought her to California, and started a family. This Perkins was going to be somebody!

But God interrupted John's plans. Visiting the church his young son attended, John accepted Jesus Christ, the living God who changes lives. He began reading the Bible for the first time. Discipled by others, he began speaking and preaching in both black and white churches. And then God told him to go back to Mississippi to help young people like himself who were going nowhere. It wasn't easy to return to the South in the 1960s—and at one point, it nearly cost him his life.

Today, John Perkins is known as a man who puts the Gospel to work. In Mississippi, he began Mendenhall Ministries and Voice of Calvary, ministering to the whole person. In California, his vision for transforming people and communities has taken shape in the Harambee Family Christian Center and the Christian Community Development Association (CCDA), bringing blacks and whites together in partnership for the sake of the Gospel. Now back in Mississippi, John is developing the Reconcilers Fellowship Training Center, which sponsors a variety of conferences for reconciliation and development. Reconcilers Fellowship publishes *Reconcilers* magazine.

Wisdom

ONE SMALL PUSH FOR JUSTICE

The white farmer looked twelve-year-old John Perkins up and down. "Can you do a man's work? I need help getting this hay in afore it rains."

"Yes, sir!" John said. John's family were sharecroppers, and he knew how to work hard. But this was his own chance to earn some pocket money. He wondered how much the man would pay, but he didn't dare ask. The going rate for a day's work in Mississippi in 1942 was a dollar and a half—maybe two.

John threw hay bales into the wagon with all the muscle he could muster. Sweat poured down his back. By the end of the day, the hay had been hauled from the field, stacked, and covered.

Standing in the man's kitchen, John waited expectantly.

"Here's your pay," said the farmer, holding out a couple coins.

A dime and a nickel—fifteen cents.

John just stood there. It was so unfair! He knew he'd hate himself if he took it. But he was afraid not to take it, afraid the man would call him an "uppity nigger" and other white folks would give him a hard time for "not knowing his place."

He took the fifteen cents.

John was angry as he scuffed his way home. Why was the man able to cheat him like that? He realized that the man had the "capital" (the land and the hay) and the "means of production" (the wagon and horses). All John had to offer was his labor. So it was the man with the capital and the means of production who made the money and set the price.

It was John's first lesson in economics, and he didn't forget it. When he was fourteen, he and his cousin Jimmy took a job for a white farmer who was considered fair-minded. The boys agreed to clear a pasture of bushes and undergrowth for a gallon of syrup and a meal per day. It was hard, back-breaking work, and by noon the boys were ready for that hot meal. But when they appeared at the house, the man's mother-in-law handed out a plate of "leavings" (table scraps).

The boys looked at each other. No way could they work all day for a few leavings. They put down their tools and went home.

When the farmer heard what had happened, he came to the boys' house and urged them to come back. He'd make sure they got a square meal if they'd finish the job. The boys agreed. John later said, "It was my first small push for justice."

Determined to use his knowledge of the way the economic "system" worked to better himself, John went to California as a young man and got a job in a new factory. His crew came up with ideas to streamline production, which made more money for the company. Then John helped organize the workers into a union so that the workers could cash in on the increased money the company made. That success felt good!

But then God got hold of John Perkins and changed his life. Eventually, he left a good job and a nice home in California to return to Mississippi to share the Gospel, bringing spiritual hope to the poor. He also used what he knew about economics not for his own benefit, but to bring economic hope to poor communities.

Wisdom is knowledge that is used in God's way.

FROM GOD'S WORD:

Are there those among you who are truly wise and understanding? Then they should show it by living right and doing good things with a gentleness that comes from wisdom (James 3:13).

LET'S TALK ABOUT IT:

1. Why didn't twelve-year-old John want to take his fifteen-cent pay?
2. How did John make what he learned about "economics" work for him? work for God?
3. Talk about other kinds of human knowledge that can become spiritual wisdom.

Forgiveness

BEATEN IN THE BRANDON JAIL

The voice on the telephone was crying. "The highway police arrested Doug and the students and took them to the Brandon jail!"

Rev. John Perkins put the receiver down and looked at his wife, Vera Mae. "I've got to go to Brandon and do something," he said quietly. "We've got to take a stand against these false arrests and beatings in jail."

Perkins had already been in jail once—just before Christmas, when he and other folks from Voice of Calvary Ministries in Mendenhall, Mississippi, went to see a black teenager who'd been put in jail. They'd heard he'd been beaten. The whole group had been "arrested"—including children—but they were never told what the charges were. Vera Mae and others from the community went to the jail, but they felt helpless and didn't know what to do. In 1969, black folks in Mississippi felt powerless against the whites who controlled everything.

That's when John Perkins got the idea for a boycott in Mendenhall. Whites owned everything—but they depended on black folks to buy from their stores. If blacks refused to buy, maybe the white folks would listen to what blacks wanted: justice, fairness, and jobs.

The boycott started at Christmas and continued for several weeks. It got the attention of the store owners all right. It also made a lot of the whites mad.

Now it was February, and Doug, a white volunteer at Voice of Calvary, was driving some Tougaloo College students back to their campus in the next county. They had just been on a peaceful boycott march in Mendenhall. The highway patrol pulled over the van and arrested Doug and the students on a false charge. They were going to teach these boycotters a lesson! Doug was beaten severely on the way to the jail.

When he got the phone call, Rev. Perkins gathered a few men and drove to the next county to see if they could post bond for Doug and the students. But when they got out of the car in Brandon, they were promptly thrown in jail. And then the kicking and beating began. . . .

Several deputy sheriffs and highway patrol officers went to work on the "troublemakers." John and his friends were slapped, punched, stomped on, and kicked in the head, ribs, and groin. Though his face was bloody and his eyes almost swollen shut, John could see the faces of the officers, twisted with rage and hate.

But for some reason, John couldn't hate them back. He didn't want hate to do to him what it had done to them—make them vicious, angry, and capable of any kind of cruelty and injustice.

It was a long time before John Perkins could see a police officer and not feel fear and bitterness. But in time he was able to forgive them because he understood that racism hurts everyone.

Racism hurt black folks because they were treated with disrespect and denied the same rights as white folks. But the sickness of racism hurt white people, too—even churchgoing Christians—by making them believe they were better than black people. Racism made it seem okay to treat blacks unfairly, even violently.

No, John realized, hating back wasn't the answer. Only the love of Jesus could change people's hearts. Jesus told His disciples to "love your enemies." Even on the cross, while being tortured to death, Jesus said, "Father, forgive them, for they do not know what they are doing."

Forgiveness is one way we can love our enemies.

FROM GOD'S WORD:

Jesus said, "Father, forgive them, because they don't know what they are doing" (Luke 23:34a).

LET'S TALK ABOUT IT:

1. Why did John Perkins think a boycott might be a good way to speak out against the way blacks were treated in his town?
2. What was John's reaction when he was beaten in jail, even though he hadn't broken any laws?
3. If Jesus could forgive His enemies, is there someone Jesus wants you to forgive?

Reconciliation

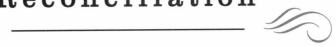

BLACK AND WHITE TOGETHER

"Rev. Perkins?" said the caller. "This is Community Legal Services here in Jackson. We're wondering if you could help us."

It was the summer of 1975. John Perkins and his wife, Vera Mae, had just moved the Voice of Calvary headquarters to Jackson, Mississippi, the year before. The work in Mendenhall—which included a church, a health clinic, and a housing co-op, among other things—had been passed on to other community leaders. But the work in Jackson was still very small. John wondered what the caller wanted.

"There's an older couple—a man and his wife—who've been living in an abandoned bread truck outside of town," the caller continued. "We're trying to find them better housing, but we need someplace to shelter them for about two weeks. Can you help?"

John scratched his head. Voice of Calvary wasn't set up for emergency housing, but . . . hadn't God called them to help the poor in Mississippi? "Send 'em over," John said. "We'll see what we can do."

When the homeless couple arrived, the staff of VOC had a surprise: The man and woman were white! Of course, John and Vera Mae knew there were poor white people in Mississippi, but because of their painful experiences with racist whites, they had largely avoided them. It was easier to minister to their own people.

As VOC staff helped rustle up emergency food, clothing, and a place to stay, John thought, *Well, Lord, you've brought me a long way since 1970 in the Brandon jail. I think you've been trying to show me for a long time that I must not only forgive my enemies and love my enemies, but that you want me to be* reconciled *and live in peace with my enemies. Black and white Christians need to work together and help each other in a* visible *way everyone can see. That is what will really show the world the power of the Gospel.*

But John knew the road to reconciliation would be long and hard. Whites who realized that racism was wrong often felt crippled by guilt. Blacks, in turn, found it easy to blame whites for all their troubles. If racial healing was to ever happen among Christians in America, they would need to get beyond *guilt* and *blame.*

For true reconciliation to happen, John knew that blacks and whites needed to respect each other as equals and partners. This would mean living near each other, working together, listening to one another, asking forgiveness and forgiving each other, and . . . worshiping together.

When Voice of Calvary Ministries established a church in Jackson, they chose to hire Phil Reed, a white pastor, and Romas McLain, a black pastor, to pastor the congregation together. Even though McLain was called to another ministry a short while later, the church remains a "cross-cultural" church, committed to bringing blacks and whites together in God's peace.

For many years the Perkinses also took their message of reconciliation and community development to California. But now John and Vera Mae Perkins are back in Mississippi—although not to retire. They're still following God's call to work for justice in the black community and to bring healing between black and white Christians.

Reconciliation breaks down the barriers between people.

FROM GOD'S WORD:

It was also Christ's purpose to end the hatred between the two groups, to make them into one body, and to bring them back to God. Christ did all this with his death on the cross (Ephesians 2:16).

LET'S TALK ABOUT IT:

1. Why did John Perkins realize it was important for black and white Christians to work and worship together?
2. In what way are blacks and whites today like the Jews and Gentiles in New Testament times?
3. How could you get to know someone better in your school, neighborhood, or work who is of another race or culture?

FESTO KIVENGERE

Africa's Apostle of Love

Bloody revolutions ripped the East African country of Uganda during the 1970s and 1980s. Especially violent was the brutal dictator, Idi Amin, who killed as many as three hundred thousand of his fellow citizens.

But God never forgets His people, and to help them through this suffering, He prepared an apostle of His love, Festo Kivengere.

Festo was born in 1919 in a beehive-shaped grass hut. He was the grandson of the last king of the Bahororo tribe, a powerful people who had ruled southwest Uganda for nearly two centuries. Festo grew up worshiping spirits and caring for his father's large herd of cattle in the surrounding lion country.

"Long before the missionaries came to Africa," said Festo, "my people knew there was a God. And we wanted Him; we desired Him. We knew

He was the Creator, and so we tried to worship Him." But they did not know how, so they worshiped all kinds of spirits.

Then when Festo was about ten, an African missionary came to his village and built a mud-hut church. He invited the young boys to join his morning classes and learn to read. Festo learned quickly and went away to high school and finally college.

But when he came home years later to be a teacher in his village, he no longer believed in God. But God still cared about Festo. A revival had started in East Africa, and people were going everywhere telling others about Jesus. But the most amazing thing was that people were confessing wrong things they had done to one another and trying to make them right.

This shocked Festo. Religious people usually only pointed out other people's sins. It made Festo think, and finally he became a Christian, too.

Confessing sin and becoming brothers and sisters together in Christ became the core of Festo's ministry. In time, Festo Kivengere became the Anglican Bishop of Kigezi and strengthened the church with deep love.

When Idi Amin tried to stamp out all the Christians in his country, the church remained strong even though many believers died. Festo and his wife had to flee the country, but he wrote a book titled *I Love Idi Amin*. He explained, "On the cross, Jesus said, 'Father, forgive them, because they don't know what they are doing.' As evil as Idi Amin was, how can I do less toward him?"

When Amin was finally thrown out of the country, hatred remained between the people. Until he died of leukemia in 1988, Festo did much to help heal the wounds left by the war.

Surrender

NO PLACE TO HIDE

When nineteen-year-old Festo Kivengere returned home after studying to be a teacher, he was surprised at what was happening in his village. Everyone seemed to be talking about Jesus and asking one another for forgiveness. He found this upsetting. *Why don't they keep their religion to themselves?* he complained.

People were singing and repenting in the marketplace, on the road, with their neighbors. There was no escape.

Finally, Festo went to his uncle the chief. His uncle agreed. "This new kind of religion is dangerous. It invades your privacy. You have no place to hide." In the days to come, the chief tried beating those who spoke openly about Jesus. But still, in the evening's quiet, one could hear nothing but Jesus songs floating on the breeze. And in the morning, as the smoke from the cooking fires drifted through the village streets, sounds of the same joyful songs accompanied it.

So the chief arrested twenty Christians and sent them off under guard to the district commissioner. But on the way, the joyful believers converted the guard to Jesus Christ. The guard came back singing like those who had been arrested. What was the chief going to do?

One day, the chief was sitting on his porch with the village elders when a wealthy cattleman came by. His servants were driving eight fine cows before them. All the elders turned to admire the cattle. "Fine-looking cows," called the chief.

"Your Honor," said the rich man, "they are yours. I have brought them back to you."

"What?" said the chief. "I don't recall losing any."

"Well, sir, a couple years ago when I was looking after your cows, I told you there had been a raid by our enemies, and four cows were taken. Do you remember?"

"Yes," said the chief.

"There was no raid," said the cattleman. "I stole them. They had calves, so now there are eight, and I am returning them to you."

"Who discovered this?" asked the chief, frowning.

"Jesus did, sir. You can put me in prison or beat me, but Jesus told me to return them to you, and I am at peace."

The chief was astonished. "If Jesus did that," he said, "who am I to put you in prison. Leave the cattle and go home."

A couple days later, the chief said to Festo, "I must admit, some great power is at work here."

Festo knew that it was Jesus. His twelve-year-old sister and his fourteen-year-old niece had been telling him about Jesus and begging him to go to church. Finally, Festo went, but he was embarrassed when the whole congregation prayed for him. Festo was so angry that he walked out and got drunk.

On his way home, he met a friend who said with great excitement, "Festo, three hours ago Jesus came into my life and forgave my sins. I want you to forgive me, too." And then he named three things for which he wanted forgiveness.

This was too much for Festo. There was no place to hide from this Jesus. When he got home, he knelt by his bed and cried, "God, help me!" And he gave his heart to Jesus.

Surrender is saying yes to Jesus.

FROM GOD'S WORD:

"Here I am! I stand at the door and knock. If you hear my voice and open the door, I will come in and eat with you, and you with me" (Revelation 3:20).

LET'S TALK ABOUT IT:

1. Why did the cattleman return the cows to the chief?
2. Why do you think Festo wanted the Christians to keep their religion to themselves?
3. Why is it good to say yes to Jesus but wrong to say yes to evil things?

Repentance

A LANGUAGE ANYONE CAN UNDERSTAND

As Festo Kivengere walked up the dusty path to his stepfather's house, he could see a scowl on the old man's face. "What do you want?" snarled the man from where he sat.

For years, Festo had hated the old man and had refused to talk to him. But he knew that must change.

In Festo's village, many things had changed because of the Gospel. A customer surprised the Muslim shopkeeper when he came in and said, "Here are two hundred shillings. I cheated you out of this money. But Jesus has changed my life and wants me to give it back. Please forgive me."

Another Christian went to a government official and said, "Here is a cow to pay my back taxes. I have cheated the government for years, but now I want to make it right."

Another said, "Here, sir, when I worked on the road crew last year, I stole this shovel. Please take it back."

"But why do you bring it back?" asked the road boss.

"I was arrested, sir."

"By whom?"

"By Jesus. He changed my life."

Even Festo's uncle, the old chief, finally gave his life to Jesus. Afterward, he paid back thousands of shillings and many head of cattle to the people he had falsely fined.

Festo also had some things that needed changing. And one of them was his relationship with his stepfather.

When he was ten years old, his father had died of tuberculosis, and his mother had married this man. But he proved to be cruel and often beat Festo's mother. Finally, Festo had to help her and the children move out and live on their own. Not long after that, Festo's mother died, and he had to see to the care of the children himself. Those experiences created great hatred in Festo's heart.

Then one day as Festo prayed, God told him to go and forgive the man. "But I didn't do anything," protested Festo. "He started it all. Besides, he's not a Christian and hasn't repented for beating my mother and ruining our lives."

"Nevertheless," said God, "all broken relationships break my heart. Go and do your part to mend it." Knowing God's heart was broken humbled Festo and made him sad.

Now he stood anxiously on the dusty path wondering what would happen. "Stepfather," he said carefully, "for years I have hated you. But Jesus has taken that hate away."

The old man squinted his eyes, uncertain whether to believe Festo. Finally, he admitted, "Yes, well, I always knew you hated me."

"You knew only a little. I came to tell you the whole story and say that it is over. Please forgive me."

The old man waved Festo closer, and together they sat and talked. An hour later, the man arose, put his arms around Festo, and forgave him. Festo was overcome. He never expected such a reaction, but he later wrote, "Love is a language anyone can understand. The barrier was gone, and we became friends. Now our homes are open to each other."

*Repentance is letting your heart be broken
over the things in your life that break God's heart.*

FROM GOD'S WORD:

[God] says, "I live in a high and holy place, but I also live with those who are sad and humble. I give new life to those who are humble and to those whose hearts are broken" (Isaiah 57:15b).

LET'S TALK ABOUT IT:

1. Why did Festo hate his stepfather?
2. What made Festo's stepfather forgive him?
3. Is there anything in your life that makes God sad?

Love

"I LOVE IDI AMIN"

One bishop's death this week is enough for us," said the frightened believers in the town of Kabale. "Remember Peter! With the help of God's angel, he escaped Herod. So go. Go now!" they urged Festo. "You can help us more from outside the country if you are alive than if you die here."

So Bishop Festo Kivengere and his wife, Mera, didn't even return to their house to get their clothes. They left everything and drove toward the mountains, expecting each moment to meet Idi Amin's soldiers at a road block.

Things had gone from bad to worse in the recent weeks. Amin was killing everyone he thought might be against him. Tens of thousands had already died. Several days before, Amin's soldiers had broken into the home of Festo's friend Archbishop Janani Luwum at one-thirty in the morning and taken him away. Then word came that he had been killed—and Festo was next on Amin's hit list.

But these frightening events did not stop Festo from preaching the Gospel. He said, "Living in danger, when the Lord Jesus is the focus of your life, can be freeing. For one thing, you no longer worry about your safety because you have none. It's all in the Lord's hands."

But it did seem wise to escape if that was possible. Idi Amin's men had already been to his house three times that day looking for Festo. And they had captured and tortured one of his ministers, trying to get the man to tell where Festo was.

As Festo and his wife fled through the night, their Land Rover was stopped by someone standing in the middle of the road. "Go through the forest," the stranger urged. "There's a roadblock up ahead with soldiers waiting to catch you." So they turned off the road and nearly drove off a cliff in the dark before they got back on the road beyond the roadblock. Finally, they arrived at the end of the road and had to continue the last five miles up the mountain by foot. Nine thousand feet up, they reached the border and safety just as the sun rose.

It was easy to hate such an evil man as Idi Amin for causing such suffering and forcing them to leave their home.

But later, as Festo prayed, God said to him, "Can you forgive Amin?"

"No, Lord."

"Suppose he had been one of those soldiers who nailed me to the cross. Do you think I could have prayed, 'Father, forgive them, all except Idi Amin'?"

"No, Master," admitted Festo in prayer. "You would have forgiven even him."

"Then you must do the same, my son."

Some time later, Festo wrote a powerful book, *I Love Idi Amin.* In it he describes the power of love to forgive even the most evil enemy.

Love means forgiving even those who don't deserve to be forgiven.

FROM GOD'S WORD:

"If you love only the people who love you, what praise should you get? Even sinners love the people who love them. . . . But love your enemies, do good to them. . . . Then you will have a great reward" (Luke 6:32, 35a).

LET'S TALK ABOUT IT:

1. Why did Festo and Mera flee Uganda?
2. What caused Festo to realize that he needed to forgive and even love Idi Amin?
3. Describe a time when you acted in love toward someone who had been mean to you.

RICKY AND SHERIALYN BYRDSONG

Coaching Kids in the Game of Life

Ricky Byrdsong was only fifteen when he met Sherialyn Kelley on a blind date on Christmas Day, 1972. The six-foot-six basketball player was smitten with the athletic Sherialyn, who was smart as well as pretty. The high school sweethearts both graduated from Iowa State University and were married on October 6, 1979.

Ricky started coaching college ball immediately after graduation in 1978. His nineteen-year coaching career took him finally to Northwestern University in Evanston, Illinois, as head basketball coach.

Sherialyn, too, was "Coach Byrdsong" at the University of Arizona, coaching women's basketball at the same time her husband was coaching men's basketball there. When the kids came along, Sherialyn became an at-home mom but continued to coach sports at her kids' schools.

Both Ricky and Sherialyn made serious decisions as adults to live for Christ. Ricky realized there was a lot more to life than just playing basketball. Coaching became a way to teach life principles of discipline, following the rules, cooperation, a positive spirit, and learning from mistakes. Win or lose, Ricky was always a role model of integrity and a man of faith.

Meanwhile, God was using Sherialyn to coach others in worship and the study of God's Word. While Ricky was head coach at Northwestern University, Sherialyn became the praise and worship team leader at The Worship Center, a church with a vision to unite persons of many races in Christian worship

When a losing streak cost him his job at NWU, Ricky began working on a book that had been gnawing inside him—a book for parents about "coaching kids in the game of life," using sports metaphors to teach parents how to encourage and guide their children.

Then he was offered a job—not as a university basketball coach, but as vice-president of community affairs for the Aon Corporation. His job description? Developing programs to help underprivileged youth reach their full potential. Speaking in schools and bringing inner-city kids to his "Not-Just-Basketball Camps," Ricky was doing what he did best—coaching kids in the game of life.

Then . . . tragedy. On July 2, 1999, while jogging in his suburban neighborhood with two of his children, Ricky was shot and killed by a young white supremacist during a two-state shooting spree. People nationwide were stunned by his murder.

Suddenly Sherialyn, only forty-two, was a widow with three preteen children. She was at a crossroad. She could give in to despair, bitterness, and self-pity . . . or she could believe that God's love is stronger than hate. In the media spotlight since her husband's murder, she has turned tragedy into triumph through public witness to her faith in God and by establishing the Ricky Byrdsong Foundation. The Foundation seeks to address the growing epidemic of violence in our society by providing opportunities for young people that instill a sense of self-worth and purpose and develop respect for others.

The torch has been passed from one Coach Byrdsong to another.

Advocate

WINDY-CITY PANHANDLER

James Saunders sized up the tall, good-looking black man walking briskly up Wacker Drive and decided he looked like a good mark. "Got a dollar or two, mister?" he called out. Unlike some of the other panhandlers in downtown Chicago, James knew he wouldn't get snide remarks like "Get a job, buddy." Not many people could pass by the wheelchair of a double amputee without throwing *something* into his hat.

"Sure," said the tall man, digging out a five-dollar bill. "Say, losing your legs must be tough. What happened?"

James was surprised. Most people just dropped in the money and hurried off. Not many stayed to talk.

It was the first of many talks on the corner of Wacker Drive and Monroe. James told his new friend, who introduced himself as Ricky Byrdsong, that he'd been stabbed in the back at age twenty-five, which paralyzed him from the waist down. An infection in his bones took off first one leg, then the other. For the past twenty-five years he'd been in and out of hospitals, had married three times, and held piecemeal jobs.

Ricky Byrdsong told James he used to be the head basketball coach at Northwestern University " . . . until I got sacked a year ago." He laughed ruefully. "Nobody would hire a coach with a losing streak. Didn't think about panhandling, though. . . . You make good money on this corner?"

James laughed in spite of himself. The tall man was obviously well-off now. Turned out that he worked across the street at the Aon Corporation—the second largest insurance broker in the world—as vice-president of community affairs.

"Don't you miss coaching?" he asked his new friend.

Byrdsong grinned broadly from ear to ear. "James, I've got the greatest job in the world. They're actually *paying* me to go to schools, talk to kids about what's important in life, and run basketball camps for inner-city kids in the summer. Not *just* basketball, either. Kids come to camp to play basketball half the time; the other half we teach them computer skills, take them to work, try to give them a vision for something besides basketball." His eyes had fire in them. "I want them to know there are other options besides becoming an NBA superstar like Michael Jordan—which isn't very likely—or hustling drugs. I want kids to know there's dignity in education and hard work."

Dignity. Pride. That was hard to come by panhandling on a street corner, even though it put food in his stomach and helped pay the rent. There was something about Ricky Byrdsong that inspired James Saunders, made him want to "stand tall," get off this street corner, and do something with his life.

"Ricky, do you think you could help me get a job?" he asked one winter morning as the two men exchanged their usual hellos.

Byrdsong scratched the back of his head. "Can't promise anything, James. But I'll see what I can do."

Within a couple of days Ricky ushered James's wheelchair into the human resources office of the Aon Corporation. There was a job in the mailroom. Did James think he could handle it?

James could hardly believe his ears. "I'll be the best employee you've got!" he said. "I'm dependable. I'll show up here on time, even stay overtime if I need to."

"He's got *that* right!" Ricky Byrdsong chimed in. "If this guy can show up on a street corner in the Windy City every morning, rain or shine, summer or winter, without fail, you *know* he's going to show up for an inside job!"

Their laughter bounced off the walls. And James was true to his word. He didn't make as much money as he sometimes did panhandling, but Ricky Byrdsong had given him something far better: friendship and dignity.

*An advocate speaks up on behalf of someone else
who is often overlooked in society.*

FROM GOD'S WORD:

Defend the cause of the weak and fatherless; maintain the rights of the poor and oppressed (Psalm 82:3 NIV).

LET'S TALK ABOUT IT:

1. Why would a man like Ricky Byrdsong make friends with a panhandler who "worked the corner" across from the big corporation where he worked?
2. Why is helping someone get a job more helpful than just giving someone money?
3. Is there someone you pass by every day—on the way to work or school—who needs *you* to be an advocate for him or her?

Victory

FROM TRAGEDY TO TRIUMPH

H e's dead, you know," said the sympathetic voice at her elbow. Sherialyn Byrdsong stopped her prayers and stared at the intensive-care nurse.

"Dead?" she echoed in disbelief. "Dead?" How could this be happening? Not Ricky, not her big strapping husband who was so full of life. Murdered?

The screams of her children still rang in her ears: *"Daddy's been shot!"* At 8:52 on a peaceful summer evening in their quiet neighborhood in Skokie, Illinois, a lone gunman had opened fire on her husband and children as they were coming home from a nearby park. The children were all right—traumatized, but alive—but Ricky . . . Ricky was dead.

The next few days were a blur. It was Fourth of July weekend, 1999. Newscasters were saying the gunman was a white supremacist shooting at over twenty-five Jews, Blacks, and Asians in a two-state spree. The shooter finally turned the gun on himself as the police closed in. Three dead—counting the shooter's suicide—and twelve wounded.

Calls of sympathy came pouring into the Byrdsong home from all over the world. Sherialyn could barely think about *why* Ricky had been shot. Just because he was *black*? It didn't make sense! Her husband was working at a job he loved, motivating kids to become all God meant for them to be. His kids needed their dad. And just two weeks earlier Ricky had heard that a publisher wanted the parenting book he was working on.

At the same time she knew why. The stronghold of evil was in a spiritual warfare with the kingdom of God, and the Evil One had scored a victory by eliminating a man who was influencing others for good, who had gotten to the place in his life where "nothing else mattered" other than living for God.

Two days after her husband's murder, Sherialyn Byrdsong held a press conference. People who watched were impressed by her poise and dignity. "The violent act that took my husband's life is yet another clarion call to our nation. . . . Wake up, America! It's time to turn back to God. . . . This is not a gun problem, it's a heart problem, and only God and reading His word can change our hearts."

In a private sharing with her church family, she said, "In the twenty years I've been a Christian, all the Scripture I've studied and all the worship songs I've ever learned were like deposits into my heart. Now I'm making withdrawals big time."

Working with Ricky's co-writers, Sherialyn Byrdsong helped oversee his book to completion, making sure that it reflected the heart of what he wanted to say to parents.[1] A lot of her energy went into establishing the Ricky Byrdsong Foundation to continue her husband's work with youth, giving them positive alternatives to a culture of violence. All three of the Byrdsong kids ran in the Ricky Byrdsong Memorial 5K Run a year after their father was killed, an event that brought together nearly two thousand people of all races pledging themselves to work against violence and hate. And on the one-year anniversary of her husband's death, at a memorial celebration called "From Tragedy to Triumph," Sherialyn spoke to a gathering who worshiped together across racial and denominational lines, to praise the King of Kings and to commit themselves to let God's love be stronger than hate.

As Sherialyn worked through her grief, keeping her eyes not on her loss but on Jesus, she taught a series of Bible studies at her church, addressing the

---

1 *Coaching Your Kids in the Game of Life* by Ricky Byrdsong with Dave and Neta Jackson (Bethany House Publishers, 2000).

question "Is God good?" Her answer: a resounding YES. "If we understand the sovereignty of God, we'll understand it's not *about* us. It's about God!"

Some people are defeated by problems;
others understand that God has already given us victory.

FROM GOD'S WORD:

"Death is destroyed forever in victory." . . . But we thank God! He gives us the victory through our Lord Jesus Christ (1 Corinthians 15:54b, 57).

LET'S TALK ABOUT IT:

1. What do you think Sherialyn Byrdsong meant when she said that studying the Bible and singing worship songs were "deposits" in her heart, and now she was making "withdrawals" to help her through this tragedy?
2. Why do you think Sherialyn Byrdsong called the senseless murder of her husband a "wake-up call"?
3. Have you ever lost someone close to you in a tragic way? Do you sometimes wonder if God really *is* good? How can you turn loss or tragedy into triumph?

Generosity

THE MISSING SHOES

But, Dad . . . !"

"I said no, so don't keep asking. I'm not going to put out money for expensive athletic shoes just for a one-week basketball camp. What's wrong with your sneakers?"

His father's words still echoed in his head as the ten-year-old boy mingled with the other kids who had signed up for Ricky Byrdsong's summer basketball camp at Northwestern University. The gym was full of black kids and white kids, kids wearing squeaky-clean athletic shoes, tossing the ball around, shootin' hoops. . . . But he didn't see anyone else wearing a yarmulke on his head.

A tall guy holding a basketball on his hip walked over to the boy. "Hi, son. I'm Coach Byrdsong. You bring any other shoes to play in?"

The boy reddened and looked down at his muddy sneakers. He shook his head. "My dad wouldn't buy me any new shoes for camp."

The coach raised his eyebrows. "Stay right there, son," he said and walked off the floor. A few minutes later he was back, jangling his car keys. "C'mon." Puzzled, the boy obediently trotted after the coach as he headed out to the parking lot. Coach Byrdsong unlocked his Jeep Cherokee and said, "Get in."

"Where we goin'?"

"To get you a pair of shoes." The coach grinned.

The boy's eyes flew wide. "Aw, no, coach. My dad wouldn't want you to do that."

"Get in, son. If you want to play ball, you gotta have good gym shoes—and they can't go outside playing in the mud."

The boy tried a few more times to tell Coach Byrdsong that his dad wasn't going to like it, but the coach cheerfully ignored him. He asked the shoe man to measure the boy's feet and fit him with a good pair of basketball shoes. Then he pulled out his wallet, paid for the shoes, and gave the bag to the boy to carry.

Back in the car, the boy tried again. "My dad will make me bring them back."

"Don't worry about it, son. I'll talk to your dad if it's a problem." Man, those shoes felt good running up and down the basketball court. And when they took a break from doing skills and drills, the boy listened as Coach Byrdsong gave them some tips about basketball . . . and life. "What's the most important skill you can develop? A positive attitude! You got the right attitude, you're on the way to being a winner!" And "Respect! Every member of this team deserves respect. And that includes the manager and everyone else on the staff. I don't want to see any of you leaving your towel around the locker room, thinking somebody else can pick it up for you."

By the time he got home, the boy had figured out how to handle his little problem. When his dad got home from work—as CEO of a large Chicago company—the brand-new athletic shoes were safely stowed at the back of the boy's closet. They only came out in time to get smuggled to camp, then back in the closet. And when basketball camp was over, there they stayed.

A couple of years passed. It was summer again and the boy—a teenager now—was excited about the plans his family was making to celebrate July Fourth, which fell the day after Sabbath. But suddenly news was spreading like wildfire over Chicago's airwaves and newspapers: A lone gunman had opened fire on a group of Orthodox Jews walking home from Sabbath services, wounding several. Then the gunman had driven north and killed an African-American man jogging home from the park with his kids.

The man who had been shot was Coach Ricky Byrdsong.

Suddenly the teenager remembered the shoes in the back of his closet. "Dad?" he said, digging out the shoes, tears filling his eyes. "I've got something to tell you."

A spirit of generosity delights in sharing whatever we have with whoever needs it.

FROM GOD'S WORD:

You must each make up your own mind as to how much you should give.... For God loves the person who gives cheerfully (2 Corinthians 9:7 NLT).

LET'S TALK ABOUT IT:

1. What do you think the father's reaction was when he heard that Coach Byrdsong had bought his son basketball shoes—shoes the father easily could have afforded?
2. Why do you think Ricky Byrdsong left the basketball camp to buy shoes for one boy instead of just saying, "No shoes, no play"?
3. Brainstorm some ways you (and your family) can develop a generous spirit.

BEN CARSON

The Brain Surgeon They Called "Dummy"

Benjamin, you're much too smart to be bringing home grades like this."

Ben Carson was sorry to disappoint his mother again, but she just didn't understand what it was like at school. He was possibly the worst fifth-grade student in the school, and his nickname was "Dummy." For Ben, a good day was when he got someone else kicked out of class rather than himself.

"I've been praying for wisdom about what to do," continued his mother, "and I think the Lord's answered my prayer. From now on, only two or three TV programs per week—"

"Per week?" howled Ben and his brother, Curtis. "What are we going to do?"

"Oh, the Lord told me that, too. From now on you're going to read two books a week and write me a report on each of them."

"But we don't have any books."

"No problem. You can catch the bus and ride right down to the Detroit Public Library, where they have more books than you can read in ten lifetimes."

At first, Ben thought his mom was cruel and heartless, but it was the beginning of the beginning for him. Even though their family had no money, between the covers of those books Ben discovered that he could go anywhere in the world, be anybody, do anything. Instead of wanting to just get out of school and work in some factory so he could buy clothes and a cool car, Ben began imagining himself as a scientist discovering all sorts of new things.

In fifth grade, he had considered himself stupid, so he acted stupid and achieved nothing. But by seventh grade, he knew that he was smart. So he behaved and achieved like a smart person. He had moved from the bottom of his class to the top, and the same students who used to call him "Dummy" were now begging him to help them with their homework.

Of course, some of them were still caught in the "stupid" trap, so instead of calling Ben "Dummy," they began calling him "Nerd" and "Poindexter" and "Uncle Tom." But Ben had caught a vision for the future and didn't let the names bother him. Instead, he said, "Let's see what I'm doing in twenty years, and let's see what you're doing in twenty years. Then we'll see who's right."

Twenty years later, at age thirty-three, Ben Carson was named chief of pediatric neurosurgery at Baltimore's Johns Hopkins Hospital, becoming the youngest U.S. doctor to hold such a position. Three years later he made worldwide headlines by leading a twenty-eight-hour operation to separate South African Siamese twins joined at the head—the first such procedure ever to succeed for both patients.

Today he performs as many as five hundred operations per year—more than twice the number done by most brain surgeons—saving the lives of children who often have no other hope.

Ben's older brother also benefited from their mother's reading plan. Today Curtis Carson is a successful engineer.

Vision

ONE SHINY ROCK

When the teacher passed out the math quiz and Ben Carson looked at the thirty problems, his heart sank. Nothing looked familiar. He put his name at the top of the paper, guessed at a few answers, and then fiddled with his pencil until time was up. The teacher had all the students pass their papers to the person behind and then gave out the answers while the kids graded one another's papers.

The girl behind Ben handed his paper back with a big goose egg at the top—zero. He hadn't gotten even one answer right! It was what he expected, but he was tired of being laughed at as the dumbest kid in class, so when the teacher called his name for his score, he mumbled, "Nuhh-hhn," hoping she wouldn't understand.

"Nine!" the teacher exclaimed. "Benjamin, you got nine right? That's wonderful. Class, can you see what Benjamin has done? Didn't I tell you that if you apply yourself you can do it?"

Nine out of thirty wasn't really very good, but for Ben it would have been a start. But the girl behind him yelled, "None, not nine! He got *none* right. Zero!"

The class burst into laughter, the teacher got angry, and Ben wished he hadn't even gotten out of bed that day.

But a little over a year later—after Ben had been "suffering" under his mother's requirement that he cut down on TV and read two books per week—a remarkable thing happened. He was sitting in science class still feeling as dumb as ever when his teacher held up a shiny black rock with sharp edges and asked the students what it was.

No one answered, not even the smartest kids in class. Ben squinted at the rock. He had just read about different kinds of rocks and had written a report for his mother. He raised his hand and said, "Obsidian."

The teacher almost didn't notice. Then he blinked. "What did you say?"

"Obsidian. That's obsidian." Ben started to shrink down into his seat thinking he'd made a fool of himself again.

"You're right! You're right, Ben!" said his amazed teacher. "This is obsidian."

Ben gained courage. "It's formed from a volcano. When lava flows down and hits water, it supercools. The elements come together, air is forced out, and the surface becomes like glass."

Suddenly he realized everyone was staring at him in amazement. It had all happened because he had been reading books. He wasn't a dummy after all!

A vision began to form in his mind. He didn't need to be a dummy if he kept on reading books—books about science, math, history, geography, social studies, literature, art, and music. They could become his ticket anywhere.

When his mom took him to the hospital clinic for checkups, Ben heard them paging "Dr. Jones to the emergency room. Dr. Johnson. Dr. Johnson to the clinic." A vision grew in his mind: One day they'd be saying, "Dr. Carson to the operating room."

Now, as a world-famous brain surgeon, he says, "I had the same brain when I was at the bottom of the class as I had when I reached the top. It is all a matter of vision, how one sees oneself."

Vision sees what is not and knows that by faith it can be.

FROM GOD'S WORD:

This happened because Abraham believed in the God who brings . . . into existence what didn't exist before (Romans 4:17b NLT).

LET'S TALK ABOUT IT:

1. Why did Ben mumble, "Nuhhhhn," when the teacher asked what his quiz score was?
2. How did Ben know what obsidian was?
3. What is *your* vision for what you might become or accomplish someday with God's help?

Wisdom

CRABS IN A BUCKET

Peers are people your age. Often we let them have an undue and sometimes negative influence on our behavior. This started happening to Ben Carson when he was in high school. First he started letting his peers tell him what to wear. That wasn't too bad except that the clothes were so expensive that Ben had to shortchange his studies to earn money for the fancy clothes.

Then his friends began suggesting that Ben wasn't "cool" if he was inside in the evenings studying. "Hey, man, what's the matter with you? It's only nine o'clock. Why aren't you outside playing basketball with us?"

Then his peers began ridiculing Ben for getting good grades. They were like crabs in a bucket. The first time Ben or anyone else began climbing up the side to get out, the others would grab him and pull him down. If they had their way, no one would escape their "bucket" of poverty and ignorance.

Ben began letting these ideas influence him. With it came a victim mentality preoccupied with "my rights." "I began to think that the world owed me something," says Ben as he looks back on those years. "It created a bomb of anger within me, always threatening to explode if anyone crossed me.

"One day I got so angry at a friend that I lunged at him with a knife, aiming it right at his stomach. By God's grace, the knife hit his belt buckle and broke the blade without hurting him."

His friend ran off, terrified, and Ben began to shake as he realized what had almost happened. What if he had wounded or even killed his friend? He would have had to live with that guilt for the rest of his life—possibly in jail.

Ben began to understand that anger and acting out weren't making him a strong person like his peers had been saying. He was actually acting like a weak person, letting other people tell him how to act, and it had almost ruined his life. The event shook him up enough that he decided to quit letting his peers tell him what was *cool* and to start studying again.

Ben now says peers are often "P-E-E-R-S—People who Encourage Errors, Rudeness, and Stupidity. We don't want to let that happen to us. God didn't give us these incredible brains so we could go off and act like maniacs every time we think somebody is looking at us the wrong way."

Be wise! Don't let your peers pull you down like crabs in a bucket.

Wisdom will save you from evil people and bad consequences.

FROM GOD'S WORD:

Only fools despise wisdom and discipline (Proverbs 1:7b NLT).

LET'S TALK ABOUT IT:

1. Why are negative peers like crabs in a bucket? Why do you think some kids try to talk their friends out of studying hard?
2. If Ben's knife blade had not broken in his friend's belt buckle, how might his life have been different?
3. Tell about a time when some of your peers encouraged errors, rudeness, and stupidity. How did you respond? Why?

Victory

IT'S NO ACCIDENT

Some people think success is accidental good luck, like a prize you might win at a party. Ben Carson learned that success is a choice or, rather, the result of a series of choices.

When Ben's mother insisted that her boys quit watching so much TV and start reading books, she couldn't even read the book reports she required them to write (though they didn't know that at the time). She had come from a family with twenty-four children, where she received only a third-grade education. She got married at the age of thirteen, had two children, and then her husband abandoned the family. But she never felt sorry for herself, and she never allowed her sons to blame others or their circumstances for their problems.

She knew education was the only way her boys would triumph over their severe poverty. A choice had to be made between failure and success, being a victim or a victor, and she made that choice for them until they were old enough to make it for themselves.

In the last couple years of high school, Ben did well enough to earn a scholarship to Yale University, where he also did well. But when he entered the University of Michigan Medical School, things didn't go so smoothly, and before long his advisor actually recommended that he drop out. "There are other useful fields you might pursue," he suggested after reviewing Ben's scores.

Ben, however, refused to take the easy way out. The advisor then suggested a compromise: Go more slowly. Take four years to complete what most people do in two.

Should he take this advice? Ben went to his room and prayed. He knew he wasn't dumb, so he didn't want to accept a "dumbed down" way out of his problem. In Ben's prayer time, God reminded him of his strengths. Ben learned best from what he read. But he had the most trouble listening to lectures in classrooms. Unfortunately, at that stage of his medical training, most of the material was communicated by lecture in the classroom.

No wonder his grades weren't up to his usual high standards. So Ben made a decision: He would skip most of the lectures and spend that time and more reading medical books. The plan worked.

"If I had accepted a victim mentality," says Ben, "I might have told myself that, being a poor boy from the ghetto, I had too much to overcome to succeed in medical school. Why not reduce my load and forget about trying to do excellent work? But I decided not to take that route. I was intent on being a victor."

And that's what he became.

As Ben now says, "A victim walking through sand looks down and sees dirt; a victor sees the ingredients for building a castle."

*Looking for shortcuts and doing no more than
what's required just to "get by" seldom leads to victory.*

FROM GOD'S WORD:

A lazy person will end up poor, but a hard worker will become rich (Proverbs 10:4).

LET'S TALK ABOUT IT:

1. Why didn't Ben do what his advisor suggested by going into some other field or taking his classes more slowly?
2. What hardships from Ben's past might he have used as excuses for not doing his best?
3. What does it mean to think of yourself as a victim? Why is that dangerous?

List of Character Qualities

ADVOCATE
Windy-City Panhandler (Ricky and Sherialyn Byrdsong)

BOLDNESS
Taking New York (Samuel Morris)

CAUTION
"No Charge" (Charles Albert Tindley)

COMPASSION
Blow to the Forehead (Harriet Tubman)

DIGNITY
" 'Whosoever' Means You!" (Mary McLeod Bethune)
The Birth of a Dream (Martin Luther King Jr.)

DILIGENCE
No Such Thing as a Menial Task (Mary McLeod Bethune)

DISCERNMENT
The Headless Phantom (William J. Seymour)

EXCELLENCE
"When I've Done My Best" (Thomas A. Dorsey)

ENCOURAGEMENT
Take Heart! (Samuel Morris)
Snip and Stitch (Eliza Davis George)

FAITH
"But . . . Where's the School?" (Mary McLeod Bethune)

FAITHFULNESS
Many Languages, Many Gifts, One Gospel (William J. Seymour)

FORGIVENESS
The Best Way to Fight (Amanda Smith)
Beaten in the Brandon Jail (John Perkins)

GENEROSITY
The Missing Shoes (Ricky and Sherialyn Byrdsong)

HOPE
Heaven's Christmas Tree (Charles Albert Tindley)

JOY
Liberty . . . or Death (Harriet Tubman)

LOVE
"I Love Idi Amin" (Festo Kivengere)

NONVIOLENCE
The Power of Turning the Other Cheek (Martin Luther King Jr.)

OBEDIENCE
Going to the Fair (Amanda Smith)

PEACEMAKER
"Be Like Libby" (George Washington Carver)

PERSEVERANCE
"Wanted: Dead or Alive!" (Harriet Tubman)
The "Sheriff" of the Three-Masted Ship (Samuel Morris)
Two Hundred Miles by Ankle-Express (Eliza Davis George)

PRAISE
The Singing Preacher (Charles Albert Tindley)

RECONCILIATION
Washing Away the Color Line (William J. Seymour)
Black and White Together (John Perkins)

REPENTANCE
A Language Anyone Can Understand (Festo Kivengere)

RESOURCEFULNESS
Most Weeds Have a Purpose (George Washington Carver)

SACRIFICE
"Son, Take It" (Eliza Davis George)

SELF-SACRIFICE
"I'm So Happy That You Didn't Sneeze!" (Martin Luther King Jr.)

SERVICE
The School on Wheels (George Washington Carver)

SUBMISSION
"Take My Hand, Precious Lord" (Thomas A. Dorsey)

SURRENDER
Taming a Wildcat (Thomas A. Dorsey)
No Place to Hide (Festo Kivengere)

TRUST
Two Dollars for India (Amanda Smith)

VICTORY
From Tragedy to Triumph (Ricky and Sherialyn Byrdsong)
It's No Accident (Ben Carson)

VISION
One Shiny Rock (Ben Carson)

WISDOM
One Small Push for Justice (John Perkins)
Crabs in a Bucket (Ben Carson)

About the Authors

DAVE AND NETA JACKSON are an award-winning husband-and-wife writing team, the authors or coauthors of more than a hundred books. They are most well-known for the TRAILBLAZERS, a forty-book series of historical fiction about great Christian heroes for young readers (with sales topping 1.7 million), and Neta's popular YADA YADA PRAYER GROUP novels for women.

Dave and Neta bring their love for historical research to the four-volume series of HERO TALES and this special-edition *Heroes in Black History*. Each book features up to fifteen Christian heroes, highlighting important character qualities through nonfiction stories from their lives.

The Jacksons make their home in the Chicago metropolitan area, where they are active in cross-cultural ministry and enjoy their grandchildren.

Trailblazer Books

William & Catherine Booth ▪ *Kidnapped by River Rats*
Governor William Bradford ▪ *The Mayflower Secret*
John Bunyan ▪ *Traitor in the Tower*
Amy Carmichael ▪ *The Hidden Jewel*
Maude Cary ▪ *Risking the Forbidden Game*
Adoniram & Ann Judson ▪ *Imprisoned in the Golden City*
David Livingstone ▪ *Escape from the Slave Traders*
Martin Luther ▪ *Spy for the Night Riders*
Hudson Taylor ▪ *Shanghaied to China*
Harriet Tubman ▪ *Listen for the Whippoorwill*
William Tyndale ▪ *The Queen's Smuggler*

*Trailblazer Books: Featuring Harriet Tubman
and Other Christian Heroes*

*Trailblazer Books: Featuring Amy Carmichael
and Other Christian Heroes*

*Trailblazer Books: Featuring William Tyndale
and Other Christian Heroes*

*Trailblazer Books: Featuring David Livingstone
and Other Christian Heroes*

*Trailblazer Books: Featuring Martin Luther
and Other Christian Heroes*

Heroes in Black History

*Hero Tales: A Family Treasury of True Stories
From the Lives of Christian Heroes* (Volumes I, II, and IV)